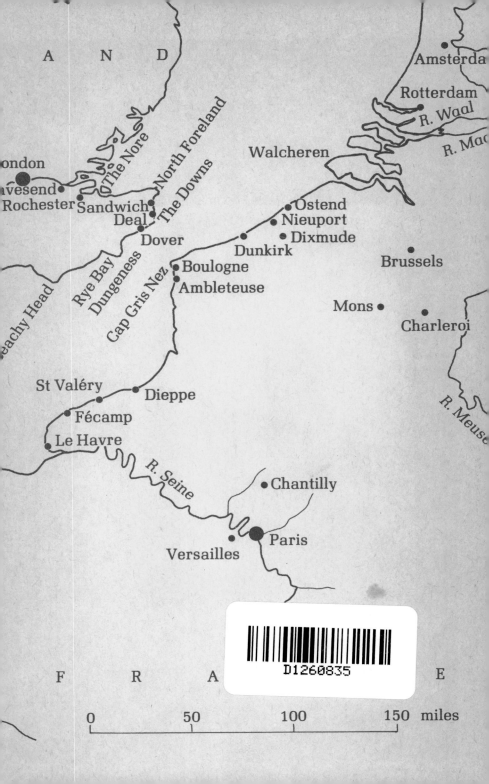

The Defeat of James Stuart's Armada 1692

Philip Aubrey

The Defeat
of James Stuart's
Armada 1692

Leicester University Press 1979

First published in 1979 by Leicester University Press
Distributed in North America by
Rowman and Littlefield, Totowa, N.J.

Copyright © Leicester University Press 1979

Designed by Douglas Martin
Phototypeset in V.I.P. Palatino by
Western Printing Services Ltd, Bristol
Printed in Great Britain by
The Pitman Press, Bath
Bound by Redwood Burn Ltd, London and Esher

British Library Cataloguing in Publication Data
Aubrey, Philip
The defeat of James Stuart's armada, 1692.
1. Barfleur, Battle of, 1692   2. Hogue, La,
Battle of, 1692
I. Title
949.2'04   D280.B/

ISBN 0–7185–1168–9

Contents

List of maps

List of plates

Preface

I wish particularly to express my gratitude to Professor Christopher Lloyd, author and naval historian, who saw some early chapters in draft, for his helpful advice and his encouragement to complete this work. Others have been equally generous in giving their time and counsel.

I am grateful for the facilities for research afforded by the Public Record Office, the National Register of Archives, the National Maritime Museum at Greenwich, the Naval Historical Library at the Ministry of Defence in London, the British Library, the Royal United Service Institute for Defence Studies in Whitehall, the Institute of Historical Research at the University of London, the Bibliotheca at Valletta in Malta, and the Camberley branch of the Surrey County Library. I acknowledge the permission of the Duke of Portland as owner and of the University of Nottingham as custodian to quote from documents in the Portland Collection. I am also grateful to the owners of the Wombourne Wodehouse papers and to the County Archivist of Stafford for authority to quote from Lord Danby's diary.

I must also thank Mrs Elsa Haigh of Camberley for assistance in the translation of some Dutch texts. The responsibility for interpretation of French sources is my own. The spelling and punctuation of quotations from contemporary documents in English have been modernized. Notes on sources for quotations have been placed at the end of the book.

All dates in the narrative are expressed in old style; that is, according to the Julian calendar in use in England till 1752. Dates expressed according to the Gregorian calendar in use on the continent of Europe were 10 days later up to 1700, and 11 days thereafter. Dates before 25 March in any year have been expressed in accordance with modern usage, with each year starting on 1 January.

Introduction

The naval campaigns of the Armada in 1588 and of Trafalgar in 1805 have been recounted many times, and are quite well known to the reading public. Half-way between them, in 1692, there took place a struggle of equal importance to the future of England, and thus of what was to become the United Kingdom, but the principal events of that year are scarcely known except to specialists in the period and those primarily interested in naval history. It is the object of this book to rescue them from the neglect they have suffered and, in showing how an invasion of England was prevented at that time, to emphasize some fundamental truths about the use of sea power by an island kingdom.

It has been the fate of England to be many times menaced by great land powers which also possessed important sea armaments. The danger of invasion by Germany was present in 1940, as it was when the confrontation was with Spain, or France, or the two in concert. What made the threat more dangerous in 1692 than at other times, was that the country was divided, for there was a certain amount of disillusion with the benefits of the four-year-old revolution. An invading army, if one could be successfully landed, stood a greater chance of popular support than at any other time. A fifth column of Jacobites stood ready to rally to the standard of the 'rightful King', and to confuse the defence by separate risings in widely dispersed places.

Louis XIV as King of France, like Philip II of Spain before him, and Napoleon and Hitler in later years, imagined that he understood sea affairs as completely as he had mastered the conduct of land campaigns. It was his personal autocratic intervention that made the defeat of his fleet, and thus the failure of the invasion project, inevitable.

In order to place the victory of 1692 in perspective it has been necessary to go back to the revolution of 1688 as well as forward to the naval and political events of 1693. The story of the struggle at sea that followed the flight of James II is of particular interest, not only to the naval historian, but also to the general student of war and international conflict. Many matters with which we are familiar in the twentieth century were already the subject of trial, of argument and of resolution in the seventeenth. The command and control of a large fleet, its relations with an allied navy, the degree to which a government might interfere in an admiral's conduct of operations, the defence of trade, the mounting of joint operations with the army, the administrative backing and finance for large naval and military forces – all these things and more find a place in this narrative.

Its central feature is the naval battle lasting six days, from 19 to 24 May 1692. It started with a fleet action off Cap Barfleur, during the course of a day and the early part of the following night, in calm, foggy weather, with two important changes of wind direction in daylight hours. The allied English and Dutch fleets were much stronger, but the French, who were under royal orders to engage at whatever odds, contrived to withdraw without the loss of a ship. Subsequently, however, 15 French ships of the line, and several smaller warships and transports, were destroyed off Cherbourg and la Hougue.

The fleet action took its name, as has been the practice throughout history, from the nearest point of land, and is known as the battle of Barfleur. The name given by the English to their later victory over the French fleet, in burning a third of its strength in ships, including nine three-deckers, was La Hogue, a spelling used in some contemporary French accounts, though the usual rendering of the name of the little Norman port is la Hougue. It is for this reason that in this book the name has either been completely anglicized to the Hogue or rendered correctly as la Hougue.

It is strange that a battle which was spectacular in itself and decisive in its results has faded so completely from the public memory. It was not always so. The action was still being sung about in the British fleet over 50 years after the event. When King William IV gave a dinner at Windsor Castle on the 145th anniversary of the battle in 1837, he surprised his guests by delivering a lecture on it.

The Admiralty has done something to keep the memory alive in names given to warships. There have been three *Hogues*: the first, a 74-gun 3rd-rate, lasted from 1811 to 1865, with screw propulsion for the last 17 years of her existence; the second, a cruiser of 12,000 tons, became all too well known when she and her consorts, the *Cressy* and *Aboukir*, were early casualties of U-boat torpedoes in 1914; the third, a battle class destroyer completed in 1945, went for scrap in 1960. There was a *Barfleur* in this class too, the fourth ship to bear the name in the Royal Navy. Earlier *Barfleurs* were 2nd-rates of 1697 and 1768, and a twin-screw battleship of 1892.

Edward Russell, the allied admiral, is even less known than the battles won under his command. His name was given to an 80-gun ship within a fortnight of the action, and there have since been three more *Russells* in the Royal Navy, the last a battleship of 14,000 tons, mounting four 12-inch and twelve 6-inch guns, sunk by mine off Malta in 1916. His most ardent admirer could not call Russell a great man; his failure to capture the imagination of the public in the manner of a Drake or a Nelson may account to some extent for the way in which his very real achievement has been forgotten. An additional reason may lie in the British preference for their fighting men to stick to being professional soldiers and sailors (and more recently airmen); they do not care for an admixture of politics – and Russell was a vigorous party man with a seat in the House of Commons.

Most general histories have relied, for a description of the crowded events of those six days, on one or both of two contemporary accounts of the battles. Josiah Burchett, Russell's secretary, was almost certainly present on board the fleet flagship, and his narrative, published 11 years after the action, has formed the basis of almost all histories in English. The best French account, written by an anonymous friend of the Marquis de Villette and included in his memoirs, was not published till 1841. These two authorities have been used in the preparation of the present text, supplemented by a study of as many contemporary sources as are readily available. Ships' logs are very uneven in their value as eye-witness accounts: some provide an excellent picture of the part played by individual ships as well as making an attempt to describe the action as a whole; others are utterly slapdash, as for example that of the *Lion* for 24 May, the last day of the encounter. 'Little wind, good weather', is all it says. 'Burnt the remainder of the ships.'

No attempt has been made to assess the importance and results of the battle since Sir John Knox Laughton marked its 200th anniversary by writing an article published in the *Quarterly Review* of 1893. Laughton, after service afloat as a naval instructor, had done much to revive interest in naval history, and founded the Navy Records Society in the same year of 1893. His article is relatively inaccessible, and it has done little to rescue the action from Mahan's devastating appraisal published three years earlier. The Hogue, Mahan concluded, was of little importance, and its results had been much exaggerated, though 'popular report has made it one of the famous sea battles of the world'. Nobody would claim that it enjoys such a reputation today.

Laughton was vigorous in his condemnation of Russell, attributing his appointment as commander-in-chief to treason, revolution and tortuous intrigue, and his success in action to superior numbers in spite of his own incapacity. This assessment appears over-harsh in the light of the evidence; perhaps this work will cause it to be modified by future historians of the period.

I shall feel well rewarded if this account rescues both battle and admiral from oblivion, and makes more people aware of events at sea in the first five years of the English revolution, and of the manner in which the Royal Navy of William and Mary made that revolution secure.

Chapter 1

Unknown: James Stuart painted about 1690, the year of his Irish campaign (National Portrait Gallery).

Revolution   *1688*

On a winter's evening in the year 1688 a tall man of 55 years of age, with a long, straight nose, full lips and a lightly cleft chin, wearing the long curled wig of the period, arrived on board a small sloop-rigged vessel at the fishing port of Ambleteuse, on the coast of Picardy between Cap Gris Nez and Boulogne. One of his attendant gentlemen lowered himself bare-headed over the side and took the passenger on his shoulders. Two French officers advanced into the breakers up to their thighs to escort him ashore, one holding the hand of the distinguished stranger.

For this was James Stuart, the Second of England and Seventh of Scotland, who had 'withdrawn' (in his own phrase) from his kingdoms 'till this violent storm is over, which will be in God's own time'.[1] He was accompanied by a young man of striking good looks. James Fitzjames, Duke of Berwick, the king's eldest child by Arabella Churchill, was said to combine something of the fine features of his grandfather Charles I with the strong countenance of his uncle John, Earl of Marlborough at this date. The vessel in which they had sailed uncomfortably from England was the yacht *Henrietta* of the Royal Navy, a navy which at the beginning of November had permitted the first successful invasion of England since 1066.

James Stuart was no stranger to exile. Forced to leave his native country in 1648 before his fifteenth birthday, he had joined the French royal army in the war of the Fronde four years later. In October 1655 he found himself excluded from France as a result of a treaty between Cromwell and Mazarin, and compelled to join the Spanish forces in the Low Countries. Although he returned to England with his elder brother Charles at the restoration of the Stuart dynasty in 1660, and rendered good service as Lord High Admiral, he had to resign from this appointment (first bestowed upon him when he was four years old) when the Test Act was passed in 1673 with the object of excluding Roman Catholics and dissenters from public office. His attachment to Roman Catholicism made him an exile for the second time six years later, after the discovery of the Popish Plot against his brother Charles II, and he spent the six years remaining before his accession at first in Brussels, later in Edinburgh.

Now, after a reign of almost four years, he was an exile once more. He fully expected that he would return again to the shores of England. He had learnt that gratitude is not to be counted upon, and had seen his army and navy desert him. Like so many of the Stuarts he failed to see his own hand in his misfortunes, and complained that 'never any Prince took more care of his sea and land men as I have done, and been so very ill repaid by them'.[2] But, given the fickle political allegiance of the English, he could have a reasonable expectation that the country would soon tire of the Dutchman who had supplanted him, and that at that moment he would be able to engineer a second Stuart restoration, perhaps with as little bloodshed as the first. This book is about that attempt and its frustration by the Royal Navy on which Charles and James himself had lavished so much care and treasure, with the able assistance of Samuel Pepys.

Pepys, nominally Secretary of the Admiralty, had become under James in all but name a minister of the Crown, with powers equal to those enjoyed in England by a Secretary of State and in France by the Minister of Marine. He was justifiably proud of his administrative achievements during his two spells at the Admiralty, from 1673 to 1679 and from 1684 to 1688; he boasted that 'the Navy of England will never be found to have been once in the good condition I have had the leaving of it twice, viz. in April 1679 and December 1688'.[3] Moreover he was so upset at its failure to prevent the landing of the Prince of Orange that he wrote and published a paper setting out in detail the state of the fleet on 18 December 1688, believing that future generations would regard the crisis between October and December of that year as of such importance that they would need a report of this nature when confronted by what happened in British waters, in spite of the fleet. He showed that there were 81 ships of all kinds at sea, including ten 3rd-rate and 29 4th-rate ships, with another seven of these rates coming forward.

It was owing to the energy of Pepys that all the repairs had been properly carried out and that neither the financial nor time limits had been exceeded. It did not occur to the English or to the Dutch, at this critical period, to consider any attempt to man and arm any ships of the 1st and 2nd rates. It was the custom to lay up the great ships from September to April, and it would have been thought suicidal to attempt to keep any of them at sea in winter conditions in the North Sea or Channel. Pepys concluded that his paper had proved the validity of three truths: first, that integrity and general (but unpractised) knowledge are by themselves insufficient qualities to conduct and support a Navy; second, that experience and integrity together cannot be depended on much more unless accompanied by vigour of application, assiduity, strictness of discipline and method; third, that it was a strenuous conjunction of all these that had raised the Navy of England from the lowest state of impotence to a lasting and solid prosperity such as the nation had never seen. But, he went on, even at its zenith it had suffered sufficient to teach us that there is something above us that governs the world.[4]

Where Pepys saw divine intervention, other men discerned the fulfilment of their own plans to replace James on the throne by one pledged to maintain the liberties of England and the Protestant religion. William, Prince of Orange, was himself a Stuart on his mother's side and was married to Mary, elder daughter of James by his marriage to Anne Hyde; Mary would inherit the throne in any event on James's death. For many years, as Stadholder of the United Provinces, William had been campaigning each summer in Flanders to keep the French out. Charles II had sent him three English and three Scottish regiments under the Earl of Ossory, a man whose fighting experience had been chiefly gained afloat. Though the earl, to whom William was devoted, died in 1680, the regiments remained in the pay of the States-General. The three English regiments were sent to defend James against Monmouth in 1685, a short diversion, but James's request for the return of all six early in 1688 had somewhat naturally been ignored, though about 35 officers took advantage of an offer that those who wished to leave might do so. The States-General, who had paid them and kept them up to strength for so long, regarded the regiments as their own. They were in any event opposed to any reinforcement of James, whom they looked upon as the last ally of Louis XIV. Two years earlier the League of Augsburg had been formed, binding the Empire, Spain, Sweden, Holland, Brandenburg, Bavaria, Savoy and several smaller principalities to act together if attacked. All continental Europe, Catholic and Protestant, was united against the French king, and William wanted the support of Protestant England in this alliance.

In 1687 William sent an envoy named Dykvelt to try to dissuade his father-in-law from policies that were splitting the country, and to sound out leading politicians of all parties. Dykvelt met them at the London house of the Earl of Shrewsbury: Halifax, Danby, Nottingham, Devonshire and others. They represented the high Anglicans and landed proprietors of the Tory party, and the City interests of the Whigs. The conversations continued with Zuylestein, another emissary from Holland, until news, made public in December, of the impending birth of a child to the Queen, altered the whole basis of the negotiations. It would have been a bold step for the Prince of Orange to anticipate James's death by placing his own wife on the throne of England while she remained next in succession. It would be quite another matter if Mary Beatrice of Modena should present the King with a male heir.

When therefore, at the end of April 1688, Admiral Russell was sent by James's opponents to Holland in order to ascertain the Prince's intentions, he was informed that William would not interfere in the affairs of England without a formal and definite invitation from a sufficient number of men of quality. The fate awaiting traitors to the Crown was well known, and had been but recently demonstrated by the failure of Monmouth's rebellion. It was therefore an act of extreme courage, born of strongly held political and religious convictions, for the men, afterwards known as the immortal seven, who signed the invitation. A Prince of Wales was born on 10 June, and soon afterwards the document was on its way to Holland in the hands of Admiral Herbert, who presented it to William on the last day of the month.

Perhaps the most seriously involved of the seven was young Charles Talbot, twelfth earl of Shrewsbury. Born in the year of the restoration, he was a godson of Charles II and named after him. He succeeded to the title at an early age, when his father died of a wound received in a duel. He had been brought up a Roman Catholic, but changed his religious allegiance after the Popish Plot. After his house had been used for the crucial meetings and the invitation had been sent, Shrewsbury mortgaged his estates for £40,000, and deposited £12,000 of it in a bank in Amsterdam as a contribution to the expenses of the coming invasion. He and Russell arrived there at the end of August.

Edward Russell, one of the two admirals in the conspiracy, was a nephew of the Earl of Bedford, later to become the first duke. He had been turned irrevocably against the Stuarts by the execution five years earlier of his cousin William, who had the courtesy title of Lord Russell, for alleged complicity in the Rye House plot to assassinate both Charles and James. Aged 35, of middle height, ample girth and ruddy countenance, he was happier dabbling in the intrigues of politics than commanding ships and men, though he had accumulated 11 years of sea experience between 1671 and 1682, had fought at Solebay, and had served in the Mediterranean under Narbrough and Herbert.

Arthur Herbert was six years his senior. Herbert did not sign the document; disguised as a common seaman, he made a safe emissary for its delivery. He was an experienced commander, who had lost an eye in action with an Algerine ship when commanding the *Rupert* in 1678, and had later been commander-in-chief in the Straits and ashore at Tangier. He had become a Member of Parliament in 1685, and had held the offices of Rear Admiral of England and Master of the Robes under James II. But in March 1687 he refused to vote for the repeal of the Test Act, and was dismissed from all official employment. He was a heavy drinker, and had other vices to match – Pepys allowed him no single compensating virtue – but it was to him that the Prince of Orange entrusted the command of the invasion fleet. Gilbert Burnet, the Scottish divine who was exercising considerable influence on both William and Mary at this period, commented coolly that he admired Providence for its trick of occasionally making use of the most unsuitable persons for the execution of great things.

Another signatory, who took across the duplicate of the invitation, was the handsome Henry Sidney. He accompanied Zuylestein, who was returning to Holland after offering the official congratulations of the Prince and Princess of Orange on the birth of the Prince of Wales, a task that would have demanded a more than ordinary degree of cynicism from any diplomat. Zuylestein, however, was not a diplomat, but a cavalryman. Moreover he was English on his mother's side; he had no compunction in forwarding the plans for the revolution. Sidney had entered the House of Commons in 1679 at the age of 38 after military service, and had later been sent as envoy to the Hague. There he gained the confidence of the Prince of Orange, but was recalled when he forwarded unwelcome Dutch comments on Charles II's policies. No doubt William was glad to see him again, and to include him in his staff for the invasion. His wife Mary had known him from childhood. Burnet admired his truly good heart and lack of malice, but admitted that Sidney was over-fond of pleasure. In fact Sidney was never more than a political lightweight, but he exerted a considerable influence on the course of the revolution. His sister was the mother of Sunderland, Lord President of James's Council and Secretary of State, who also played a part, before fleeing to Rotterdam, by persuading the king not to accept French help to repel the invasion.

The most important Tory to sign was Thomas Osborne, Earl of Danby. He had served Charles II rather too well as Lord Treasurer, and had ended in the Tower in 1679. Released on bail five years later, he had been skirmishing for political office under both Charles and James. His signature was especially welcome to Mary, who considered him largely responsible for arranging her marriage to William. Danby had considerable influence in Yorkshire, and it was for this reason that William was advised to make his landing at Bridlington or in the Humber estuary. The south-west was believed crushed by the all too recent failure of Monmouth's rebellion, and the north was better able to supply horses.

Danby could secure the support of most of Yorkshire, while two other signatories from the upper house, Lumley and Devonshire, had followings in the midland counties of Derbyshire and Nottinghamshire respectively. William Cavendish, tall and handsome, was the fourth earl of Devonshire, and was to become the first duke. A Whig, he had fought at James's side in battle against the Dutch fleet under de Ruyter. His task in the revolution was to secure Nottingham castle and its surroundings. Richard Lumley had been educated as a Roman Catholic, and had been abroad for six years before the Restoration brought him to Court. Made a baron in 1681, he had fought for James at the time of Monmouth's rebellion, when his troopers had captured the bastard duke. In 1687 he had turned against the king, resigned his commission as colonel of a regiment of carabineers, and, like Shrewsbury, had changed to the Protestant faith.

The last signature was again very welcome to Mary: it was that of Henry Compton, Bishop of London, her former tutor, who had confirmed and married her. He was the youngest son of the second earl of Northampton, who had been killed in action during the Civil War. An ambitious prelate and friend of Danby, he had become Bishop of London and Dean of the Chapel Royal in 1675. Though he possessed strong politico-religious convictions, he was by no means learned. James, who thought he talked more like a colonel than a bishop, removed him from the Privy Council and the Chapel Royal, and soon afterwards suspended him from episcopal office, spurning an appeal by Mary on behalf of her former mentor. Small wonder, then, that Compton had found himself in touch with Dykvelt, and a member of the revolutionary group meeting at Shrewsbury's house.

In spite of the military and political attractions of a northern landing, William received contrary advice from the English admirals. They represented that the south coast could not be left open to French intervention, and that, in any event, the lateness of the season made the Channel preferable to the North Sea. William was not yet ready. It was only when Louis sent his armies to the middle Rhine in mid-September that he knew himself secure from French interference at home. He placed his trust in the League of Augsburg to keep Louis occupied, and the League was in fact able to assemble 100,000 men to fight the French by February of the following year.

James, landing on the French coast with only two attendants and his illegitimate son, was no more a stranger to conflict than to exile. He had been present at Edgehill, while still a boy, to see his father's army fail to secure a victory. He had learnt the art of land warfare under Turenne, and had become a lieutenant-general before his 21st birthday. The year 1657 found him captain-general of the Spanish forces in the Low Countries, fighting against Turenne and Cromwell's expeditionary force of 6,000 men. At the Battle of the Dunes in the following year, he found himself admiring the conduct of English troops opposed to him, a sentiment that was to recur in later life.

During his brother's reign he twice commanded an English fleet in action against the Dutch – off Lowestoft in 1665 and at Solebay in 1672. He was of course aware of the preparations afoot in the Netherlands during the summer of 1688. From the end of May when he made a personal visit to the Medway and Thames defences, he maintained a squadron of about 20 ships and some fireships under Sir Roger Strickland in the Downs. It cruised across the Thames estuary to Solebay and back, and the Dutch took the precaution of sending their inward-bound convoy from the East Indies north-about instead of through the Channel. By mid-August the danger of invasion was clear, and efforts were made to reinforce Strickland to a total of 38 ships of the 3rd and 4th rates, with six of the 5th and 6th rates and 17 fireships, but they did not start joining till early October. Strickland had plenty of sea experience. Ten years earlier, as rear admiral to Herbert in the Mediterranean, he had helped his admiral to overcome the stubborn resistance of the Algerine ship when Herbert lost his eye. But he was a Roman Catholic, and in September was faced with a mutiny in his flagship after an ill-judged attempt to have Mass said publicly on board. Though he remained in the fleet as vice admiral, he was replaced in command by George Legge, Lord Dartmouth, who had earlier fought at Solebay, had been governor of Portsmouth, and had been a commissioner charged with the evacuation of Tangier. An order in council for a general press of seamen was issued on 25 September, the day after Dartmouth's appointment, though outward trade was at first exempt. The fleet was tolerably well manned by the end of October.

Dartmouth went on board the *Resolution*, captain William Davies, at the Nore on 3 October. He had only 16 sail of warships and six fireships in company. At a council of war next day it was decided that smacks should lie close to the principal buoys in the estuary with orders to remove them on a threat of invasion at Harwich or in the Thames or Medway. At Harwich itself the lights were to be altered so that any strange sail might be led aground on a shoal. Ten days later a further council decided to sail in view of the receipt of a report that the Dutch fleet was at sea, but it took ten days more for Dartmouth to reach the Gunfleet, an anchorage towards the northern side of the Thames estuary. By then, 24 October, his strength had almost doubled, to a total of 31 warships and 14 fireships. To Dartmouth, the Dutch designs appeared very desperate and ill-advised. He was certainly opposed to risking his own fleet by taking it towards the Dutch coast, and was content to despatch the three best-sailing frigates under Thomas Hopson in an attempt to gain early intelligence of any enemy movement.

James kept up a brisk personal correspondence with his naval commander-in-chief, besides issuing official instructions through Pepys. He was receiving intelligence reports from Holland, and on 14 October, his 55th birthday, passed on the gist of one dated the 6th: 'Herbert, who commands their fleet in chief, is to look you out, and observe your motions, whilst the Prince of Orange . . . is to go with his army to land.' Six days later he observed that 'I see God almighty continues his protection to me, by bringing the wind westerly again, which will give you an opportunity to get out, and hinder the enemy from coming over.'[5] But the prince had indeed put to sea on that very day of 20 October. Two days later his fleet was back in the estuary of the Maas with damaged rigging and the loss of 400 horses, suffocated while battened below hatches. He had been hindered, as James had predicted, but he was not to be deterred. News of his setback reached James on 26 October, at the same time that he learned that Dartmouth had his fleet moored at the Gunfleet.

Dartmouth was well placed to intercept a force attempting a landing in Essex or Suffolk, as he seemed to expect. But he was in no position to guard the entrance to the English Channel. Had he moved to the Downs, he would have been in the right place to dispute the passage of the Dover straits, and would also have been able to move his fleet across the Thames estuary, outside all the shoal water, had the invasion been directed against East Anglia or the Yorkshire coast.

Early on the morning of 30 October, after a night of wind from between north and north-east, Dartmouth made the signal to unmoor, and sailed on the ebb, hoping to clear the shoals by nightfall. He had no doubt that the Dutch would get to sea that day. He had his scouts out, and believed it impossible for him to miss such a fleet as William's. William did not in fact sail a second time till 1 November, and it was indeed a vast concourse of shipping: 200 transports in nine divisions carrying 15,000 troops, including the three English and three Scottish regiments, veterans of his border campaigns, and 49 warships as escort. With the wind strong at north-east there was no question of a landing on the east coast. Nor was there any idea of looking for the English fleet. The closely escorted convoy made good progress to pass Dover on the 3rd, and to reach the Isle of Wight by nightfall on that day.

While the Dutch ran before the boisterous wind through the Straits and down the Channel, Dartmouth's frigates sent cruising were driven back on the 1st, and his fleet was forced to strike yards and topmasts to ride out the gale at anchor with plenty of cable veered. On 3 November at break of day, 13 ships were sighted nine miles to windward of the English anchorage. Three frigates cut their cables, and managed to capture one Dutch fly-boat that had lost her rudder. She was carrying 290 men of Colonel Babington's regiment under a major. The men seemed glad to be taken, the officers less so.

Dartmouth's fleet was under sail at eight o'clock, and at ten received news from the yacht *Katherine* that the ships sighted had been stragglers from the enemy fleet, which had already passed. Dartmouth considered himself the most unfortunate man alive, but his fleet was still not concentrated, and he could only follow the Dutch down Channel. On the 5th, when he reported to James, he had got no further than Beachy.

William had passed Torbay and the Dart before the wind shifted westerly and obligingly carried him back again. He had with him, besides Russell, Shrewsbury and Sidney, in the person of Burnet as chaplain a man full of political wisdom and skill, with strong liberal views. It was Burnet who had drawn up the instructions for Dykvelt's mission. William's Dutch advisers were headed by William Bentinck, a man who had already served him faithfully for 18 years, and in whom the Prince placed absolute trust. The army was under the Duke of Schomberg, his services borrowed for the occasion from the young Elector of Brandenburg, who was also providing additional troops to protect the Dutch frontier. William celebrated on 4 November the 38th anniversary of his birth and 11th of his marriage. He landed at Brixham on the following day, also an anniversary, given over throughout the kingdom to anti-Papist demonstrations and thanksgiving for the timely discovery of the 'gunpowder, treason and plot' against James's grandfather.

The Dutch fleet did not linger in the open anchorage of Torbay. As it sailed it encountered five French warships. All five were taken or sunk before the fleet sought the shelter of Falmouth.

There were no reproaches from James for his unhappy naval commander-in-chief. The king replied to Dartmouth's report at once, assuring him that he was 'fully satisfied you did all that you could and that nobody could work otherwise than you did'. He was sure that all knowing seamen must be of the same mind.[6]

Anthony Hastings in the *Woolwich* had captured two Dutch ships. Apart from this trifling loss, and the fly-boat taken by Matthew Aylmer in the *Swallow*, William's entire force was able to land without opposition. All the horses were swum ashore in three hours while there was not a breath of wind. The population was friendly, but the gentry, with their three-year-old memories of the repressive aftermath of Monmouth's rebellion, were slow to declare for the prince.

William advanced warily, and the king, with the army he had kept encamped at Hounslow Heath all the summer, moved west to meet him. The prince was concerned at the possibility of his father-in-law being killed or taken prisoner. James himself was unwell, and was unable to visit his advanced forces on 21 November because of nosebleeds. After that the rot set in. Cornbury, eldest son of Clarendon, and thus as a Hyde related to Mary, was the first to defect; Marlborough, Grafton and Berkeley went over with 400 horse on the 23rd; Prince George of Denmark, husband of Princess Anne, deserted with Ormonde next night after supping at the king's table at Andover. Danby and the northern conspirators took York on the 22nd, Lumley prepared to seize Newcastle, and in the early hours of the 26th Bishop Compton organized the flight of Princess Anne with Marlborough's and Berkeley's wives from Whitehall.

The fleet had meanwhile been active but ineffective in the Channel. The *Montagu* and *Dartmouth* had collided when there was little wind off Beachy Head on 5 November, but the fleet had steered for the Isle of

Wight next day. On the 7th it was forced by a storm with rain to bear away for the Downs, the *Resolution* with a sprung foremast. Anchoring there in the evening, Dartmouth was given the news of the successful landing in Torbay. Another of his ships, the *Centurion* commanded by Sir Francis Wheeler, had run ashore opposite the South Foreland. On passage to the Downs the *Pearl* had taken a small Brandenburger vessel carrying letters and despatches from the Prince of Orange to the Hague. Dartmouth forwarded this useful intelligence material to London, but wondered whether the captured vessel was a true prize. 'Between a war not declared and an invasion made . . . I am in doubt what to do', he told Pepys.[7] On 16 November, after receiving from Pepys a report of the enemy strength as it had been a month earlier, he sailed again with the whole fleet, resolved to fight the Dutch at Torbay.

There were no enemy ships off St Helen's or in Spithead, but Dartmouth was forced to reduce his strength further by detaching the *Montagu* and *Constant Warwick* to Portsmouth for repairs. At daylight next morning, the 18th, he found that he had been set to the southward during the night, and that Alderney was but 21 miles distant. On 19 November, his numbers down to 22, he stood in for Torbay and within sight of what he took to be the Dutch fleet from the masthead. As darkness fell the weather grew worse again and drove him back to anchor at St Helen's at noon next day. On 22 November he moved the fleet to Spithead.

To James, as he turned back towards London, Dartmouth seemed one of the only men he could trust. He had with him Lord Dover, who had been attached to him since the Restoration, and whom he had raised to the peerage on his accession. It was Dover whom he dispatched from Andover on the 25th with verbal directions about the safety of the Prince of Wales, who had been brought to Portsmouth on the previous day and saluted with 21 guns from every ship. The preservation of his heir, whatever became of himself, became an obsession. On the 29th, back at Whitehall, he told Dartmouth to get his son 'sent away in the yachts for the first port they can get to in France', but changed his mind before sealing the letter and instructed the admiral to keep the prince safe and have all things ready for him to embark at the proper time. Two days later he judged that the time had come and gave orders for his son to be sent away; at nine in the evening of the same day he wrote again to stress his impatience to know that Dartmouth had received his instructions and put them into execution.

To the admiral this seemed the height of folly; after discussing the matter with Dover he replied on 3 December that they had resolved between them not to do anything. Writing still from the *Resolution*, he pointed out that obedience to the king's orders would be treason to His Majesty and the known laws of the kingdom. To send the prince away without the consent of the nation would be inadvisable at any time, but at this moment, with a French destination, it was likely to prove fatal to the king's person, crown and dignity. Dartmouth ended by reminding his royal master how prophetically he had foretold all his misfortunes. It was France that Dartmouth saw as the enemy. The presence on French soil of a pretender to the English throne would entail on posterity a perpetual war and provide a standing temptation to the French monarch to 'molest, invade, nay hazard the conquest of England' – a remarkable piece of foresight.[8]

The fleet still gave an appearance of loyalty: on 1 December all the flag officers and captains at Spithead had signed a memorandum in which they thanked God that the king had decided to call a parliament, a step constantly urged by Dartmouth, and the paper had been carried off to London by one of the captains, John Berkeley, himself a peer though very distantly related to the earl mentioned above. But it was too late. The prince was hazardously conducted overland to London, and Dartmouth was not called upon to adopt the alternative plan of providing convoy for a yacht to Margate and thus up the Thames. On the 10th the queen and her infant son were finally despatched to France, and James took his decision to withdraw. He told Dartmouth that he had been basely deserted, that there was an infection amongst those still with him and that the same poison had manifested itself in the fleet, as Dartmouth had himself admitted. His hopes for the future were already pinned on Ireland, and he instructed any of the fleet that would stick to him to go there. This news caused Dartmouth almost insupportable grief and anxiety, but he ignored the invitation to attempt to salvage part of the fleet for further service to James in Ireland.

The reason is not far to seek. Two days earlier he had received his first communication from the Prince of Orange. It had been written as early as 29 November, and invited him to join the fleet under his command to the prince's. William could not believe that Dartmouth would contribute towards the destruction of either the Protestant religion or the liberties of England. The admiral sent his reply at once by hand of Captain Aylmer, putting himself and the fleet of England under His Highness's gracious protection, believing it a just and commendable act to join him. When he received from a distracted Pepys a memorandum signed on the 11th by 23 Lords Spiritual and Temporal, who were in effect the interim government of the country, instructing him to prevent all acts of hostility and to remove all Popish officers out of their commands, the die was already cast. George Churchill, like his brother Marlborough, had been an early defector by taking over the *Newcastle* to a new allegiance. It was said afterwards that he and Aylmer had planned to seize Lord Dartmouth so as to bring over the whole fleet. Strickland resigned his command on the 13th, followed by the other Roman Catholics. Berry was promoted to vice admiral in his place, and Berkeley to rear admiral.

The Prince of Orange learned at Windsor on the 16th that the fleet was his, and ordered Dartmouth to leave 13 ships and two fireships at Portsmouth under Berry, and to bring the rest to the buoy of the Nore. The prince told the admiral that he desired to see him when he had complied. His order reached Dartmouth on 19 December, but after two days of calm the wind came easterly again. Dartmouth did not reach the Downs till 1 January and finally anchored at the Nore on the 11th.

Although the queen and Prince of Wales had crossed the Channel successfully, James was apprehended, insulted and brought back to London. There was nothing for him to do but to try again, and nobody attempted to stop him. In Burnet's phrase, pity had taken the place of indignation. He remained just over a week at Rochester, but on 23 December he and Berwick had gone.

Berwick, although only 18 years of age, had played a part in these events, having been in command of the Portsmouth garrison at the critical period. On the king's orders he went to join the army at Salisbury, but returned to Portsmouth when James turned back to London. His garrison of 3,000 men lacked a store of provisions, the militia held the Portsdown hills commanding the land exit from the port, and the fleet blocked the sea. A victualler from Southampton was seized by Berry, now Dartmouth's second-in-command. When Berwick went to see the admiral to complain, Dartmouth told him with tears in his eyes that he could do nothing. He was an admiral in name only: the fleet was no longer loyal to the Crown. Berwick surrendered the port on the king's orders and joined his father at Rochester.

The eyes of father and son, as they came ashore in France, were directed not on the troubles that lay behind them but on the future, for James considered that he had only withdrawn 'so as to be within call when the nation's eyes are opened'.[9] It was Christmas Eve according to the calendar in use in England, though ten days later by that used on the Continent. After their rough and cold passage they were in no mood to celebrate the feast. They obtained post horses at an inn, and next morning they took the road, James to rejoin his wife and infant son at St Germains, Berwick to wait on the French king at Versailles to report his father's arrival and to request asylum.

Chapter 2

Unknown after Kneller: William III in state robes with the collar of the Garter. The artist has effectively concealed the king's lack of stature (National Portrait Gallery).

Consolidation *1689*

William had inherited a naval establishment that possessed, by the standards of the age, a sound administration and a good fighting force. Sailing ships of the era, their measurements dictated by the sizes of timber available for building, were remarkably similar in appearance, whatever their origin. Individual ships sighted at sea could not be recognized as hostile, friendly or neutral, even by practised seamen's eyes, until their colours could be made out, so that the ruse of false colours was often successful when tried. Russell, attending a meeting of the Admiralty Board in February 1692, asked for the issue of French colours to all his vessels of the 4th rate and smaller. The largest ships, those of the 1st rate, had three gun-decks mounting a total of about 100 guns. The three-decker had been introduced in the French and English navies in the 1630s, and the first English ship of this type, the famous *Sovereign of the Seas*, was still afloat and in the fleet as the *Royal Sovereign*. The sides were of English oak, two feet thick; masts and yards were of fir, pine or spruce. Riga was considered the best source of supply, but New England pine was then being used for the masts and bowsprits of the English fleet. The smallest ships to lie in the line of battle carried 50 guns and were classed as 4th rates.

The muzzle-loading cannon was a most inaccurate weapon: the ball was not a close fit in the barrel; the thickness of the metal at the touch-hole varied from gun to gun, giving different time intervals for ignition of the gunpowder charge; the movement of the ship, particularly rolling, added to the difficulties of accurate laying. A single hit caused a hole no more than eight inches in diameter; it could easily be stopped by the carpenter. But a number of shots closely grouped could cause large and jagged holes, potentially dangerous if close to the water line, just as continuous bombardment on land could breach a wall of masonry. Nevertheless these wooden ships were almost unsinkable by solid shot. Damage aloft and heavy casualties could reduce them to floating wrecks, and in single-ship or minor actions they were often surrendered on this account. Given the protection of the line of battle a damaged ship could haul out of the line to repair her spars and rigging and to plug holes on the water line by careening, that is by listing the ship so as to bring them clear of the water. The carpenter and his mates could then get to work. In the three fleet actions covered by this account, those of Bantry Bay, Beachy Head and Barfleur, not a ship was lost by either side while the line held.

The decisive weapon was the fireship. All ships were built of highly combustible material; if one caught fire, the danger of an explosion of the abundance of gunpowder was very great. Fireships had dispersed the Spanish Armada off Calais 100 years earlier, and they were still capable of causing havoc amongst anchored ships.

It was very necessary for the clumsy ships of the time to anchor in order to hold their positions in the tidal streams of the Channel. In light or contrary winds this meant spending six hours under weigh followed by six hours at anchor so as not to lose all or much of the distance gained under sail. The English called the practice 'stopping the tide', the French '*étaler les marées*'. The technique was to play an important role in the actions between them.

Their high sides and built up sterns allowed these ships to be forced easily to leeward. Rigged with square sails, they could not in any event be steered closer than three points, almost 70 degrees, off the wind. Tacking was a slow, cumbersome and laborious business, requiring many men on deck to brace the yards round and to sheet the sails home. Jibs and staysails had not yet made an appearance; the bowsprit carried a square sail, sometimes two, similar to those on the fore, main and mizzen masts.

Manning the fleet presented a perennial problem to the Government. To get it to sea usually meant placing an embargo on movements of merchant shipping, with consequent disruption of trade, and loss to the commercial community. It further meant giving authority to captains of ships and to justices to press men for the royal service. Much of the business at meetings of the Admiralty Board was taken up with providing protection from impressment to particular classes of seamen whose employment was considered as important to the nation's welfare as the manning of the fleet. Then there was the posting of captains, lieutenants and warrant officers (masters, boatswains, gunners, carpenters, pursers, surgeons), usually on the recommendation of somebody who had the ear of a Commissioner. Naval and military ranks were still interchangeable – though the commander-in-chief was appointed as an admiral he was still often referred to as 'the general'; commanding officers of ships, though usually called captains or commanders, often retained the rank of colonel, Hastings and George Churchill being two examples.

At that time, as throughout the history of this country, there were those who were more interested in fighting the class war than any wider conflict. There was agitation in favour of the 'tarpaulins', officers who had risen by merit to command, usually after gaining their early seagoing experience in merchant vessels, as opposed to the 'gentlemen', who sometimes owed their preferment as much to friends in high places as to their own efforts. The criticism was exaggerated, both as to numbers and in substance. In June 1692, after the battle which forms the centre of this narrative, the commander-in-chief declared that 'though great noise has been made that the fleet was officered by gentlemen', there were not more than ten captains and not one lieutenant.[1] In a fleet of some 60 ships of the line, with attendant frigates, galleys and fireships, this was a small proportion, and gives the lie to a paper produced over a year later seeking to show that 'there hath been negligence, ignorance or treachery' on the part of the Lords of the Admiralty and the Navy Commissioners in discharging their trusts.[2] This polemic opened with the bald statement that the captains were not bred to the sea but were chiefly land officers, and went on (as its 41st point) to allege that admirals had been selected more for their service as pages than as seamen. This argument, like many of its kind based more on envy than fact, ignored the sea service, first as volunteers, then as lieutenants and finally in command, endured (and it not too harsh a word) by all those of gentle birth who reached the higher ranks in the Royal Navy of William and Mary. Some may well have owed early promotion to their interest at Court or with a member of the Board, but to pretend that they were ignorant of sea affairs is nonsense.

Largely thanks to the work of Pepys, the Navy represented the largest industry in England. It was a huge importer of raw materials from the Baltic and North America: it sustained large ship-building and ship-repairing yards; it made substantial purchases of agricultural and clothing products; every summer it hired up to 50 victuallers to keep the fleet supplied; it paid, fed and provided medical care of a sort for up to 30,000 men. The Navy Board was responsible for the ships and men, the Commissioners of Victualling for provisions, the Commissioner for Sick and Wounded Seamen for hospitals. Another similar body, the Commissioners for Transport, provided sea transport for troops. The Treasurer of the Navy drew £3,000 a year, an enormous salary reserved for politically acceptable holders. Lesser officials of the Navy Board were the Comptroller, Surveyor and Clerk of the Acts.

The employment of the fleet was in the hands of five Commissioners since the duties of Lord High Admiral had been put in commission. At the head of all was the Secretary of the Admiralty; Samuel Pepys, whatever his feelings about his 'late Royal (but most unhappy) master's retiring', remained at his post, and soon picked a quarrel with Dartmouth for applying direct to William for orders.

Russell, who was still in attendance on the prince, was more circumspect. 'His Highness has commanded me to let you know,' he wrote to Pepys on 4 January 1689, ''tis his pleasure that you forthwith order to the buoy of the Nore to my lord Dartmouth, if there, or to the commander-in-chief, that all the fleet remains at the Nore till further orders, of which I will wait on you tomorrow and discourse further.'[3] There had been a hard frost since before Christmas, but on 8 January, while Pepys was with William at St James's, they saw through the garden windows that a thaw had set in with a change of wind. Rain was falling, and the fleet was ordered in for the winter. New dispositions were decided four days later at a meeting attended by William, Herbert, Pepys and Russell. Twelve ships and three fireships were provided for the Mediterranean, six for the Channel, eight for Ireland; all the rest were to reduce to the lowest possible complement without paying off.

William had started to give orders as if he ruled the country when still outside its capital. But the revolution had left the constitutional lawyers, and above all the Anglican divines, with a problem about the succession that had to be solved, and solved quickly. Danby, arriving in London from Yorkshire on 26 December, found that on Christmas Eve the Prince of Orange had been invited to assume the executive government until the Convention met on 24 January, an invitation accepted three days after Christmas. Danby at once saw the princess as an essential ingredient of any settlement, and wrote on 4 January urging her to come over 'for the Prince's interest as well as your own (and above all for the nation's sake).'[4] The same thought had occurred to others, and Pepys was soon directing Herbert to take the yacht *Fubbs* across to Holland to fetch her.

By the time she arrived at Greenwich, after a smooth crossing to Margate – 'the sea was like a looking glass', she wrote – escorted by the Dutch admiral Almonde, the legal arguments whether James had abdicated or had deserted the throne had been settled between the two houses of Parliament, and the succession conditions and oaths had all been embodied in a Declaration of Right. William had made his own position quite clear: he would be neither regent nor consort; he would be made king for life or he would return to the Netherlands. Mary, though a strong personality and four and a half inches taller than her husband, had equally made clear her feelings to Burnet months before: there could be no question of her ruling as queen; she had not imagined there could ever be an occasion when the husband had to be obedient to the wife. And so on 13 February, in the banqueting house at Whitehall from which Charles I had stepped to his execution only 40 years previously, William and Mary jointly accepted the Crown of England, as William III and Mary II.

Pepys had served loyally through the interregnum, and now it was time for him to resign. He was almost 56 years old. There was of course a successor as Secretary of the Admiralty, but his replacement as naval adviser to the Crown had to await William's choice of Secretaries of State.

William lost no time in choosing his council, with Danby (soon afterwards created Marquis of Carmarthen) as Lord President, Halifax as Lord Privy Seal, Mordaunt and Godolphin as members. Nottingham and Shrewsbury were the Secretaries of State. It was a judicious mixture of Tory and Whig. Shrewsbury, still only 29 years old, was diffident about accepting so high an office; Nottingham on the other hand took up his duties with relish.

Daniel Finch, eldest son of the first earl of Nottingham, had been elected a Member of Parliament in 1673, and had served as a Lord of the Admiralty for five years from 1679, during which time he moved to the upper house on succeeding to the peerage. It was this Admiralty experience which led him to consider himself an expert on naval affairs, and thus automatically to his assumption of responsibility for them. A Tory of strong principle, loyal to the Established Church, he was one of the last prominent political figures to accept the revolutionary settlement. Though he could not agree that William was the lawful king, he comforted his conscience with a text from holy scripture: 'In the day of his power the people submitted unto him.' Now aged 41, he suited William well.

The revolution was not given long to establish itself. A month after the accession, the French admiral Gabaret with 14 ships of the line, eight frigates and three fireships, all flying English colours at James's request, crossed to Ireland from Brest at the second attempt, and landed James at Kinsale.

The new king did not take the close personal interest in naval affairs to which the Admiralty and Navy Boards had become accustomed under the later Stuarts; his Dutch fleet, though composed of separate contingents from the maritime provinces, was managed efficiently by de Wildt of Amsterdam without his intervention. When Herbert got to sea again in April, he sometimes received orders from the king countersigned by the Secretary of State, at other times from the king countersigned by the Admiralty, and occasionally from the Admiralty signed by the Commissioners. The lack of uniformity was dangerous, and inevitably produced misunderstandings. The firm control of James, and the administrative genius of Pepys, were being sorely missed.

William was, however, alive to the urgent necessity for co-ordination between the two fleets. One of his first acts on reaching St James's was to ask the States-General to send over three deputies, whom he named, to negotiate a naval agreement with Nottingham, Herbert and Russell, whom he nominated as the English deputies. They met for the first time at Herbert's house on 19 March. A total joint strength of 80 ships for the Channel and Mediterranean, with ten frigates on patrol between Dover and Walcheren, was quickly agreed, and the Dutch acquiesced in English insistence on the command of the joint fleets, since English numbers would always predominate in an agreed ratio of five to three. The written agreement, 'of concert of the fleets of England and Holland', though dated 29 April, was not finally signed till 25 May.

The plans looked fine on paper, but two months had by then elapsed since James's landing. Herbert found only five ships of the line and one fireship ready at Portsmouth on 18 March, while no Dutch ships appeared before early June, and the last in mid-July. William was at first reluctant to authorize a general press and embargo on trade, the two well-tried methods of manning royal ships, with the result that the fleet heading for Irish waters to interrupt James's communications with France was undermanned as well as being too small for the job. It was not till 15 April, when Herbert was already at sea, that an embargo was placed on shipping in order to man the fleet; even then, colliers, coastal shipping, fishing vessels and trade with Holland were excluded.

The fleet sailed on 4 April, and was off Cork by the 12th. Herbert regretted that he had not been ordered to embark the two regiments for which he had asked; with them he was confident that he could have retaken Kinsale, the possession of which he considered 'of mighty importance'. The port was at that moment lightly defended; its reduction at a later date would almost certainly cost 'much blood, time and money'. Herbert was thinking of the value of the place to the French for supplying or withdrawing their troops, but Sir Robert Southwell had told the king early in the year, before James had set foot there, that the southern Irish ports in hostile hands were 'more prejudicial to the trade of England than either Salee or Algiers ever was'.[5]

James had meanwhile been consolidating his hold of Ireland. The Holy Roman Emperor, asked for the assistance one Popish prince might expect from another, returned a dusty answer, as might have been foreseen, from one in a league pledged to overthrow the king of France. Louis himself provided 400,000 crowns, but his offer of troops was rejected by James, who said that he would recover his dominions with his own subjects or perish in the attempt. James had landed with only a small following of English and Irish nobility, 100 French officers and about 2,500 mixed troops. But Tyrconnel, whom he had appointed viceroy two years earlier, met him at Cork and brought an army of 30,000 foot and 8,000 horse to his standard, an action that brought the reward of a dukedom. Soon Londonderry and Enniskillen were the only two Protestant footholds in all Ireland. Before the end of April the 68-year-old diarist John Evelyn noted in London: 'There now came certain news of King James's being not only landed in Ireland, but . . . absolute master of all that Kingdom. . . . This is a terrible beginning of more trouble.'[6]

James might have exploited this early success by crossing to England or Scotland, but the French advised him not to attempt such a thing. Gabaret had returned to France, keeping well to the westward in order to avoid any Anglo-Dutch fleet, and leaving three frigates at James's disposal. The French were perhaps uncertain of their ability to transport and supply a military force in the face of the naval opposition they must expect. This naval opposition at last made its appearance at the end of April.

Although the States-General had declared war on France in February, England had not yet done so, though the French ambassador had been sent packing the moment William reached London. Neither fleet seems to have shown any hesitation on that account, however, to open fire when they met. Château-Renault, the French admiral, had 24 ships; Herbert, who had been forced to shelter in Milford Haven from 23 to 26 April, had only 18 when he sighted the French entering Bantry Bay on the last day of the month. Château-Renault's fleet brought 1,500 men, with money, arms and ammunition, in support of James, and had started landing them at the head of the bay when Herbert stood in boldly next day.

The French weighed, and a running fight ensued, first on one tack and then on the other, in the confined waters of the bay. It was indecisive; when the French broke off the action late in the afternoon in order to return to the anchorage, Herbert's ships were too damaged to follow, and his casualties had been heavy. The French sailed for home on 5 May, but they ignored Rooke with four ships and a yacht bound through St George's Channel to guard the crossing between England and Ireland.

George Rooke, who makes his first appearance in this narrative at this point, was just under 40 years old, and three years older than Russell, who was later to become his commander-in-chief. As a boy he had shown a tendency towards petty theft, causing his father to pack him off from his home near Canterbury to serve under the Restoration admiral Sir Edward Spragge, preferring, as he said, to hear of his son being drowned at sea, rather than to have him hanged on land. Rooke had adapted well to life afloat, and was now an experienced captain, charged with the important tasks of sustaining William's two remaining footholds in the north of Ireland, and of convoying the army of reoccupation.

Herbert sent Aylmer ahead with his report of the action, and himself reached Plymouth on 7 May and Spithead on the 12th. Château-Renault snapped up seven Dutch merchant vessels homeward bound from the West Indies as he crossed the Channel approaches on his way back to Brest. He narrowly missed Killigrew in the *Dragon* with only one other escort to the English homeward convoy from the Mediterranean.

Though honours clearly rested with the French, who had not been prevented from accomplishing their mission, and whose communications with Ireland were still open, both sides claimed a victory at Bantry Bay. James, when told of the defeat of the English fleet by the French, is reported to have exclaimed peevishly that it must be the first time ('C'est bien la première fois donc'). But he recognized his opportunity. He pressed the French ambassador to keep the French fleet in Irish waters, so that it could take control of the north channel, carry guns for the reduction of Londonderry, and transport James and his army to Scotland, where he was assured of a welcome. Château-Renault could then retire north and west of Ireland so as to avoid interception by the strong allied force that these operations were sure to provoke. It was too late, however; Château-Renault had gone.

In returning directly to France, without any attempt to exploit the advantage he had gained over the English, Château-Renault was giving expression to the principle underlying all French naval operations for many years to come. The mission was the important thing to keep in mind; a commander must not be deflected from his responsibility for accomplishing it. Château-Renault came from a noble family established near Blois on the Loire. He had seen plenty of action against the Barbary corsairs and against the Dutch, and had been made *chef d'escadre* over 15 years earlier at the age of 36. He would have been most upset had he been openly accused of lack of initiative, and he was certainly hurt when his king damned his achievement at Bantry Bay with the faintest of praise.

William, who badly needed a victory of some kind, went to Portsmouth on 15 May, made Herbert the Earl of Torrington, knighted his subordinates Ashby, who had led the van, and Shovell, who had commanded the *Edgar*, and ordered a gratuity of ten shillings a head for the seamen. For Torrington it was as much a reward for his part in the revolution as for the brush at Bantry Bay.

The allied fleet began to build up its strength with English and Dutch reinforcements, and it was soon time to divide the English into red and blue squadrons. Russell had entered Parliament as the Whig member for Launceston, but William contrived to remove him from the political scene at this time by appointing him admiral of the blue. For another danger was now threatening the allies: the French had seen correctly that the decisive theatre for naval operations was going to be the Channel; Louis had ordered his Toulon squadron under Tourville to move to Brest, and it sailed from Hyères before the end of May.

Anne Hilarion de Constantin, at that time known as chevalier de Tourville, had been born in 1642 in the Normandy town from which his family derived their name and title. Destined for the Order of St John of Jerusalem, he was made a knight of the Order when four years old. In 1660 he joined, as a volunteer, a 36-gun frigate fitted out at Marseilles for service with the Order, and sailed in her to its headquarters in Malta. Soon afterwards he was in action with Turkish ships off Cape Matapan, and severely wounded. From 1667, like other Frenchmen who gained their early seagoing and fighting experience in the Order, he had a successful career in command of French royal ships and squadrons in the Mediterranean, reaching the rank of lieutenant-general in 1682. His delicate features and almost feminine appearance concealed strong nerves and almost reckless courage. Moreover he was a complete master of his profession.

He had now received orders from the king to take a fleet of 20 ships corresponding to the English 2nd, 3rd and 4th rates through the Straits to join Château-Renault. Accompanied by the marquis de Villette, another experienced admiral now beginning his twelfth sea campaign, he set out by coach to Avignon, and thence by water. With six frigates, eight fireships and four storeships, his force numbered 38 sail. Persistent north-west winds met it after it had passed Cape St Vincent, forcing Tourville to sail well out into the Atlantic in order to weather Cape Finisterre. Although the allied fleet under Torrington lay for six weeks mostly within nine miles of Ushant, as Russell was later to explain to a critical House of Commons, Tourville slipped past it, aided by the weather, and entered Brest on 20 July. He had been two months at sea, and his ships had almost run out of water.

The marquis de Seignelay, fire-eating Minister of Marine, who was on board Château-Renault's flagship, moved across to the *Conquérant*, a new ship equivalent to an English 2nd-rate, which carried Tourville's flag. Seignelay had long experience of naval administration, in which he had been well schooled by his father, Jean-Baptiste Colbert, one of France's greatest ministers, who had died in 1683. He was greatly elated to see the magnificent fleet created by his father, and longed to be present at a great naval victory.

The orders issued by Louis to his minister this summer are of particular interest, since they express for the first time the doctrine of 'the fleet in being', a doctrine which the English Crown failed disastrously to appreciate in the following year. If Tourville were successful in joining the Brest fleet, it was never to go to sea, but always to give the appearance that it was about to sail. This, wrote Louis, was the surest way of preventing the enemy from doing anything worthwhile against his kingdom. Only if there were an enemy descent on the northern coast of France might his ships enter the Channel.[7] The royal commands did not suit Seignelay, who despatched a stream of letters urging the king to send the fleet into the Channel.

The allied fleet, now composed of 34 English and 20 Dutch ships of the line, with four frigates and 17 fireships, left its blockading station on 27 July for a rendezvous with victuallers, subsequently cruising south of Kinsale so as to prevent succour from reaching Ireland. There on 13 August intelligence was received that the French fleet was at sea. It had been sighted on the 7th well clear of Ushant, but steering south.

Tourville had indeed sailed on 29 July, and had stood south-west into the Bay of Biscay in order to exercise his fleet, thus posing no immediate threat to England or to English communications with Ireland. Torrington took no chances, and covered Rooke by patrolling south of Waterford. There was a single-ship action between scouts of the opposing fleets in which the English ship *Portsmouth*, commanded by George St Lo, was taken and later blown up to avoid recapture. It was the end of the season, and both fleets returned to harbour. Seignelay, who had remained on board the French flagship, was suffering from a chest ailment, and was landed at Belleisle before Tourville went back to Brest.

By the time the allies reached Torbay at the end of August, Torrington had lost nearly 600 dead from scurvy, and had a mounting sick list approaching 2,500 – casualties equal to those of a major action. All that was required to prevent outbreaks of scurvy on board ships on lengthy voyages was a regular issue to the men of lemon or lime juice. This had been proved at the beginning of the century on the first expedition organized by the East India Company to Sumatra and Java, when the crew of one out of four ships escaped being stricken, because the captain provided lemon juice and insisted on regular daily dosage. It is one of the mysteries of seafaring that scurvy continued to incapacitate and kill sailors for the next 200 years or more.

While Torrington and Russell were agreed that the fleet ought now to proceed to Spithead in order to recuperate, while ships of the 3rd and 4th rates were detailed for the winter squadron, the king and Nottingham were worried about Ireland, and did not wish the fleet to go any further to the eastward. On 2 September William ordered Torrington to prepare for sea and to report what ships could be spared to escort a Straits convoy and when they could sail. He also asked whether Torrington could attempt to capture Kinsale with three regiments already in the west country.

Two days later William introduced a further political requirement: Princess Anna Maria of Neuburg had married King Carlos II of Spain by proxy, and William desired to accede to the demand of his ally that the English fleet should bring her to her new country. William nominated Russell to command the escort, specified a 2nd-rate as a suitable vessel for Her Majesty, and suggested Santander as the destination. The queen was to be brought by a yacht furnished by the States-General from Düsseldorf to Rotterdam.

Torrington and Russell discussed these requirements and replied on 7 September. They did not care for Santander because it lay too far into the Bay of Biscay; they suggested Corunna. The escort to the Straits convoy could then provide additional protection to the queen, whose personal escort could consist of seven ships, four of the 3rd and three of the 4th rate. 'We think a 2nd-rate very improper', they wrote.[8] Finally they told Nottingham that the fleet could not sail despite the king's orders; there had been 40 more deaths in the last three days. The operation against Kinsale must wait. Russell sent, in addition, a personal protest that seven ships did not constitute a suitable command for an admiral, in spite of the honour of escorting the Queen of Spain. He recommended Ashby in the 3rd-rate *Berwick* for the job.

When William repeated his orders for the fleet to sail for Brest it did so, only to be driven back next day into the shelter of Torbay. It was not till 28 September that the king accepted that the French fleet was back in harbour, and agreed that Torrington might come to Spithead and then to London. With Torrington's flag hauled down and Russell summoned to Whitehall, the command of the fleet at Spithead devolved upon William Davies, vice admiral of the red. But the king insisted on further cruises to the westward. They were carried out by an Anglo-Dutch squadron under Berkeley, rear admiral of the red, who returned to Plymouth on Christmas Eve and to Spithead in mid-January. Although the Kinsale operation had to be abandoned after the troops had embarked, the continuous naval presence in the western approaches had the effect of isolating James, of protecting Rooke from interference, and of covering the trade. It was not done without loss. In a violent storm at Plymouth on Christmas Day, two warships were lost, one English and one Dutch, together with three French prizes.

It had been a disappointing summer for the main fleet, but there had been small but significant successes elsewhere. The squadron in Irish waters, effectively screened from French intervention, had been active in attempts to succour Londonderry. The little *Greyhound*, a 6th-rate, approached the beleaguered town on 8 June, and found that a boom had been laid across the river Foyle. She grounded and was severely handled by artillery before she was refloated. She had to go to Greenock for repairs.

The relief force of three regiments (2,000 men) under Kirke reached the entrance to Lough Foyle a week later. Percy Kirke had been governor of Tangier in 1682 and, with Pepys and Dartmouth, had arranged its evacuation two years later. He had fought for James as a brigadier against Monmouth at Sedgemoor in 1685, but owed to the new king his promotion to major-general. He had a reputation for shortness of temper and roughness of speech.

On 19 June, in ignorance of the dismal condition to which the garrison and townspeople had been reduced, a council of war decided against any attempt on the boom. Instead it was agreed to occupy the island of Inch in Lough Swilly to the west of Londonderry. Fortunately an attempt was made at the end of July to relieve the town by forcing the boom. John Leake, who had distinguished himself in command of the *Firedrake* at Bantry Bay, and had been promoted to command the *Dartmouth*, was selected for the task. The men of the *Swallow*'s longboat hacked a passage through the boom for the *Dartmouth*, which then anchored off the castle and engaged it, while two victuallers passed through. The wind dropped, and the longboat's crew completed a good day's work by towing the leading victualler to the quay at Londonderry. On 31 July the enemy raised the siege and marched away; next day the Enniskillen garrison, which Kirke had managed to re-supply, broke out. The tide had turned in northern Ireland.

Rooke meanwhile was busy preparing to convoy an army of ten regiments of foot (6,000 men) under the Duke of Schomberg in 80 transports from Hoylake to Carrickfergus, and successfully accomplished it in August. A further 40 transports with horses and stores followed. The only naval setback in these waters had occurred on 10 July, when the Scottish Navy lost two small frigates, the *Pelican* and *Janet*, both captured by James's three frigates when they boldly appeared off the Mull of Kintyre. At the end of the season Rooke worked down the Irish coast, his sails being seen by James off Dublin, though the weather prevented any attack. He sent four ketches raiding into Cork harbour, and reached the Downs on 13 October.

Another little naval episode of this summer deserves mention. Two small French frigates from Dunkirk were commanded by two remarkable but quite different men. The larger vessel, of 24 guns, was under Jean Bart, an illiterate blond giant in his 39th year, who had learnt the arts of sea warfare privateering under the Dutch, and had transferred his allegiance to France in 1672. In the French navy officers such as he, who owed nothing to aristocratic influence and everything to their own professional competence gained in command of privateers, were known as *officiers bleus*, and wore blue breeches. The rest, who formed the majority, came from noble families and wore red breeches; Forbin, who commanded the smaller vessel, of 16 guns, was a notable example. Six years younger than Bart, this young nobleman from Provence had recently returned from the Far East, where he had been for a time Admiral of Siam.

After successfully escorting a convoy from Dunkirk to Brest, the pair of them set out from le Havre with another convoy and encountered the *Tiger* and *Nonsuch*, both credited by the French with 50 guns, although the *Nonsuch* only carried 36. Bart was persuaded by his aristocratic junior against his own judgment to give fight, but both French frigates were overwhelmed by the superior force against them and compelled to surrender. The two captains were carried to Plymouth; Forbin, stripped of his fine clothes, had been rigged out in a waistcoat instead of a shirt and 'a great pair of breeches, with a hole on the left buttock'.[9] The Governor of Plymouth had them lodged under guard in a tavern. Forbin was soon able to raise 500 crowns to meet their expenses, and sent off a report on the action to Seignelay and a request for exchange to Schomberg. A bribe to a seaman from Ostend produced a file to cut through the iron bars of the window, while a friendly surgeon arranged for a Norwegian wherry to be moved to a quiet part of the harbour and pro-

visioned for a cross-channel voyage. After 11 days in captivity the two
captains let themselves down from the window of their lodging by their
bed-sheets at midnight, and rowed out through the anchorage to sea and
to freedom. It was a sad day for England when two such intrepid
scourges of merchant shipping were allowed to escape.

William's eyes were still on what he considered the main theatre of war,
the land campaign on the Continent, and he had chosen to despatch
Marlborough, with 8,000 experienced troops, not to Ireland, but to serve
in the Low Countries under the command of the Prince of Waldeck. Two
treaties were signed between England and the States-General in August:
the first was short, and covered little but an agreement to stop trade and
supplies to and from French ports; the second was a treaty of amity and
alliance. In December England acceded to the treaty between the Emperor
and the States-General, signed at the Hague in May. William, who had
been unwell in the spring, recovered his health after passing the summer
at Hampton Court; he and Mary moved back to Kensington in October
and opened their first Parliament. Alterations to Kensington Palace,
which had been bought from the Earl of Nottingham, were not complete,
and the court was temporarily established at neighbouring Holland
House till Christmas time. Throughout the autumn William had to endure
a stream of complaints from his general in Ireland.

The army, under the elderly but experienced Schomberg, was a mixture of French Huguenots, newly raised English regiments, Dutch and
hired Danish troops. After the initial success of capturing Carrickfergus,
Schomberg had advanced south to Dundalk, where his way was blocked
by James's army. He could not advance along the only road, with bogs to
the right and left, nor could the army be sustained if it moved away from
the coast. He wanted shoes for the men and horses; the arms were poor,
the troops failed to look after them, the cannon were ill cast. He complained that he lacked staff and reliable senior officers; he could not find
a cavalry officer fit to be employed as a brigadier; the cavalry officers took
no care of their troopers' horses and were astonished at the lack of inns at
which to lodge. Officers were constantly asking for leave to return to
England. The artillery evoked his strongest criticisms: its officers were
ignorant, lazy and timorous; he never before saw so many bad officers.
Compared to professional Continental armies, in which English and
Scottish regiments had served with distinction, the English component
of Schomberg's army in Ireland was evidently of a very low standard.
Among the French he discoverd 120 Papists and had them arrested and
sent back to Hoylake. Even so the French battalions were stronger than
the English. While Dutch and Huguenot troops suffered little from
disease, English casualties from this cause were very high. It is small
wonder that William decided in January 1690 that he must go to Ireland
himself.

Chapter 3

Unknown after Wissing: Mary II. An earlier portrait adapted to suit the queen's advancing years (National Portrait Gallery).

Defeat   *1690*

Russell's first attempt to cross the narrow seas from the Downs to fetch the Queen of Spain in his flagship the *Duke* ended in failure, so he shifted his flag to the yacht *Fubbs*, and sailed in her with five escorting warships on 11 December. A month later Evelyn was lamenting the stormy weather: 'What mischief it has done at sea, where many of our best ships are attending to convoy the Queen of Spain, together with a thousand merchants laden for several ports abroad, I almost tremble to think of.'[1] All the ships were in fact safe enough at that time, for although the queen had embarked on 18 December, bad weather had kept the ships and yachts in harbour ever since. On 2 January 1690, after 16 days of the queen's company, compelled to occupy a tiny cabin measuring six feet by three feet and situated below the water-line, the admiral was near the end of his patience. The queen had neither money nor credit, and the 212 persons of her suite were all being accommodated on board the yachts and ships of the escort at William's expense. Like many a seaman before and after him in moments of stress, Russell hoped that 'this, as all other things, will have an end, that I may go to my poor dwelling in the country, thank God for my deliverance, and never so much as look towards salt water again'. When he heard, a few days later, that a French squadron was waiting in Dunkirk to intercept him, he confessed that he would 'as lief be in the Bastille as here'.[2]

The reported French squadron turned out to be no more than three small privateers, the weather eased, and Russell was able to move the queen and to shift his flag back to the *Duke* in the Downs on 18 January. A week later, to the thunder of salutes from ships and forts, Russell came into Spithead, where a vast concourse of shipping was assembled: Killigrew and Almonde with the allied squadron for the Straits, Wright with six 4th-rates to escort the West Indies trade, and over 200 merchant vessels awaiting convoy. The Duke of Norfolk, representing King William and Queen Mary, came to call on the new Queen of Spain; Prince George of Denmark and Princess Anne paid their respects.

Contrary winds continued to hold up the convoy, driving it back to Torbay on 23 February and again on 2 March, and it was not till 7 March that Russell finally sailed for a nine-day passage to Corunna. Russell with nine ships sailed ahead of the convoy, which consisted of over 400 ships under the English, Dutch, Danish and Swedish flags, with a few from Hamburg and Lübeck. Killigrew, additionally charged with preventing further French reinforcements from reaching the Channel from the Mediterranean, had ten ships on the starboard side of the convoy; Almonde, who was under Killigrew's command, had 15 Dutch escorts on its port side. There had been no convoy to Leghorn and Smyrna the previous year, so the Levant company had seized the chance to send double cargoes. Even so, under powerful stimulation from Seignelay, French influence in Constantinople was growing at the expense of that of England and Holland, and exports of English cloth did not reach the volume of earlier years.

When Russell arrived off Corunna on Easter Sunday the folly of risking a great ship in winter was again demonstrated. The *Duke*, taken into Ferrol by a local pilot, was driven aground. The Queen of Spain landed on 27 March, but it was another month before Russell, having sent on the *Duke* to serve as Killigrew's flagship, returned in the *Suffolk* to home waters. He turned over the command of the blue squadron to Delaval, his newly promoted rear admiral, and hastened back to resume his political life in the capital. As early as 9 February he had asked Nottingham to move the king to dispense with his services afloat for the coming summer; his health, he wrote, was not in too good a condition, his affairs in much worse.

The strength of the main fleet for the summer of 1690 had been decided as early as 5 January; it was to consist of 40 ships. With a Dutch contribution in the agreed ratio of five English to three Dutch, the total fleet in the Channel should therefore be 64. The bulk of the English contingent would be 3rd-rates, but there would eight great ships of the first two rates and seven of the 4th rate, besides 27 smaller vessels and 20 fireships, the whole requiring almost 35,000 men. It was a tall order, and the priority given to convoy escorts for the Mediterranean and West Indies delayed the refits of the Channel ships.

Torrington, who resigned from his post at the Admiralty at the end of 1689, afterwards asserted that he had admitted to Nottingham that he was afraid 'now in winter, whilst the danger may be remedied', and had warned him: 'and you will be afraid in summer when it is past remedy'.[3] At the end of January, before he left for Spain, Russell was writing to Nottingham: 'For God's sake, my lord, cast your eye some time towards the next summer's fleet. I dread the French being out before us.'[4] In spite of these warnings, the French were ready first. Captain St Lo, who had been wounded and was a prisoner at Brest, later confessed himself amazed at the speed of fitting out French ships. He remarked that a ship of 100 guns was ungunned in four or five hours with greater ease and less hazard than in England, where the operation took at least a day to complete.

The first task for the French was to reinforce James with over 6,000 troops and supplies, landed at Kinsale and Cork. The escorting squadron of 27 ships under d'Amfreville sailed from Brest on 7 March, the same day that Russell left Torbay for Corunna. Three days later Russell had a report that the French fleet had passed ahead of him. Each fleet was intent on its own design and not seeking an action, though the French managed to take a couple of English merchant vessels on passage. After landing the French troops d'Amfreville had to embark five Irish regiments in exchange, as part of an agreement between Louis and James. He left Cork on 17 April and somehow again missed Russell, this time homeward bound, during his passage to Brest.

William was busy preparing for his departure to Ireland and making arrangements for governing the country in his absence. Mary had hitherto taken no part in affairs of State during her 11 years in Holland, nor during her first year on the throne of England. She possessed a strong character and an exceptionally alert conscience. Politicians, who as always judged others by their own standards, considered that she suffered from an excess of goodness and simplicity. Her own concern was to avoid cutting a foolish figure in the world, for she saw clearly that monarchs were invariably classed as very good or very bad. William could do no more than constitute a strong Council of nine to advise her when for the first time she exercised the duties of monarchy.

The Whig interest was represented by Devonshire, Dorset, Mordaunt (who had been made Earl of Monmouth in 1689) and Russell. The latter, offered a renewed appointment as admiral of the blue, had pleaded ill health as his reason for declining it. The five Tories were headed by Carmarthen. Marlborough was there for military advice, but where the Council was particularly strong was on the naval side. There was not only the seagoing experience of Russell, Devonshire and Monmouth, but also the administrative skill of Nottingham and Pembroke, a former ambassador at the Hague and now First Lord of the Admiralty. Mary had scarcely a good word to say for any of them. She did not like Carmarthen, nor trust Marlborough; Nottingham's loyalty was still suspect, others were weak, or obstinate, or lazy; Pembroke and Monmouth were mad. Even Russell, who had been most highly recommended to her, had obvious faults.

William's attempt to govern through a coalition had failed; he had been forced in February to accept a moderate Tory administration under Carmarthen. The Tories on Mary's council were also members of Carmarthen's government, from which Shrewsbury, the last Whig, resigned as Secretary of State on the eve of William's departure, leaving all to Nottingham. Both houses of Parliament had opposed the king's going to Ireland; he had therefore adjourned them as soon as his revenues had been secured.

The change of government was a reflection of a mounting disenchantment in the country. The first enthusiasm for the liberties of England and the Protestant religion had faded in the constant party bickering. Halifax had resigned under the strain of acting as confidential adviser to the king. There was jealousy owing to William's partiality for foreign advisers and commanders, though Bentinck, made Earl of Portland, by tackling affairs with a toughness fed by his own ambition, was proving the mainstay of the government. Already a Jacobite underground movement was beginning to gain strength and audacity – William's lack of charm, his silent and brusque manner, made a stark contrast with the personal qualities of James.

Whatever the political stresses at home, William was determined to obtain a military settlement in Ireland so that he could be free to go back to the Continent. By 14 June he had crossed to Carrickfergus, his 288 transports escorted by six warships under Shovell. In Shovell's barge the king was rowed ashore from the yacht *Mary*. His army of 36,000 was over half composed of foreigners: it contained 10,000 Danes, 7,000 Dutch and Brandenburgers, and 2,000 Huguenots.

Shovell, born in the same year as Rooke, with whom his name was to be linked in history, had started as an apprentice shoemaker in Norfolk before being sent off as cabin boy or captain's servant to Narbrough, the English commander-in-chief in the Mediterranean before Herbert. He obtained his first command at the age of 27, was wounded at Tangier two years afterwards, and now, a further 11 years later, was generally considered one of the best captains in the fleet. As we have seen, he had been picked out for honour after the battle of Bantry Bay.

On his way north to escort the king and troop convoys, he had gone into Dublin Bay on Good Friday, and had cut out the *Pelican*, captured in the previous July from the Scots, a feat commemorated in a ballad of the period. Leaving the *Monk* in the bay, Shovell embarked in a yacht, and crossed the bar with two hoys, a ketch and some pinnaces. The *Pelican* was abandoned by her crew, and the English were able to board her and to lay out an anchor to haul her off the shore. One of the hoys ran aground during the withdrawal, but the whole force stood by her, enduring insults and some sporadic firing from the shore, until she was refloated on the next tide.

William intended to release Shovell to join the main fleet as soon as the army reached Belfast. He was fully aware that the fleet would be dangerously short until Killigrew too had returned from Cadiz. Since Russell had refused a sea appointment, Killigrew had been made admiral of the blue squadron. With Shovell, its rear admiral, also detached, the squadron was reduced to a single division under Vice Admiral Sir Ralph Delaval, third son of a Northumberland baronet, with over 25 years of sea experience behind him.

After some demur Torrington had accepted the command in chief together with command of the red squadron, and his flag had been hoisted on board the *Royal Sovereign* at the Nore on 10 May. When Torrington returned to London 11 days later, Rooke, his rear admiral in the *Duchess*, took the ships to the Downs, where he found Vice Admiral Ashby in the *Berwick*. Torrington was back from London at the end of the month; the fleet sailed on 12 June, arriving off St Helen's two days later at a strength of 45 with 14 fireships in attendance. By 22 June, when he received his sailing orders in St Helen's roads, Torrington had 34 English and 21 Dutch ships under command, and heard on that day that the French were off Falmouth with 77. He sailed on the following day, protesting that the odds were great, while Nottingham serenely informed the king that our fleet was stronger than any the French could send out, and the queen that she might expect very good success.

At the same time Carmarthen was suggesting to the king a descent by the Marine regiments on southern Ireland. The fleet was so well manned with seamen that they would not be missed. In this he was sadly out of touch with reality, for both regiments had been promised to Torrington; he was angry at their slowness to report on board, and was conducting anxious correspondence with Nottingham about the exact extent of his authority over their officers. Before Carmarthen sealed his letter to the king he reported the French fleet off Falmouth, and later off Portland. He admitted that the allied fleet was not concentrated: nine ships were at Plymouth, some in Irish waters, and seven Dutch had not yet joined. Fresh orders had been sent to Killigrew on 14 March, as Russell had suggested before he sailed for Spain, telling him not to dally at Cadiz.

Killigrew was in fact already on his way home, having failed in the part of his mission that related to French reinforcements from the Mediterranean. His squadron based on Cadiz had lost two Dutch ships in a storm, but it was still stronger than a French squadron of ten under Château-Renault when it was sighted shepherding some French merchant vessels westward through the straits. Killigrew gave chase, but was easily out-sailed. He put back to Cadiz, whence he sent on the Mediterranean trade, and sailed himself on 7 June to make a slow passage of 35 days to Plymouth, with Almonde and an Anglo-Dutch squadron of 12 escorting the homeward trade.

Tourville had accompanied Seignelay to Court at the end of the previous summer, and had left the order of St John, taking the title of count instead of chevalier. This left him free to wed, and his marriage contract to a widowed marchioness was signed by Louis XIV. More important, the king gave him command of the fleet for the coming season, promoted him to vice admiral and authorized him to fly an admiral's flag.

He started to get to sea before the end of May. Like the allied fleet with its red, white and blue squadrons, the French ships were divided into white, white and blue, and blue squadrons. Tourville commanded the white squadron, the others being under officers with the rank of lieutenant-general. Again like those of the allies, each squadron was sub-divided into three divisions, one commanded by the admiral or a lieutenant-general, and the others by officers with the rank of *chef d'escadre*. The French ships were rated in imitation of the English practice but, like the Dutch, their 1st rate included virtually all the three-deckers, carrying between 76 and 110 guns. Ships of the 2nd rate mounted 64 to 74 guns, and included a few three-decked 74s; those of the 3rd rate had between 50 and 60 guns, corresponding to the English 4th-rates and, like them, the smallest ships capable of lying in the line.

Château-Renault joined from the Straits on 11 June, and Tourville sailed on the 13th with a fleet of 76 ships attended by frigates, storeships and 18 fireships. He had to work the tides in the light summer airs, but sighted the Lizard on 20 June, sent four ships to reconnoitre Plymouth, and three days later was off the Isle of Wight with allied ships in sight.

In spite of Nottingham's and Russell's optimism in London, Torrington was much weaker than his opponent. Unable to proceed to the westward to concentrate with Killigrew and Shovell, he drifted up Channel on the flood, keeping between the enemy and his own bases in the Thames, still hoping for reinforcements of English and Dutch ships. The Dutch under Evertsen formed his white squadron, he commanded the red himself, and Delaval the blue. Torrington saw his duty quite clearly: while others were afraid of a French invasion, he always held that 'whilst we had a fleet in being' they would not make the attempt. Although the concept was not new, and the policy had been applied successfully by Louis in the previous year, and indeed by the English as long before as 1545, Torrington's neat phrase passed into the lore of naval strategy.

When he first stood towards the enemy they refused action, leading him to conclude that they were acting with caution in spite of their numerical superiority. By next day he felt glad that they had declined a battle, and was resolved to avoid fighting. A council of war unanimously agreed with his opinion, and recommended retiring, if necessary, to the Gunfleet. An action on such unequal terms could have but one result. But if the allied fleet continued to observe the French, there might be an opportunity of getting to the westward in order to join Killigrew and the other ships supposedly there. If not, Torrington told Nottingham, he would follow the advice of the council of war. Only if he were defeated would the French dare to attempt any of the many things open to them. Meanwhile ships in the river should be fitted out to join him, and those to the westward should come first to Portsmouth, and thence, if the French had stationed themselves in the Thames estuary, they might join him over the flats of the foreland.[5]

Torrington was not, however, permitted to conduct the campaign as he wished. Mary's advisers in London were pressing her to issue directions for the fleet to engage the enemy, and the reality of sea power was brought home to the queen herself when she found that, with the French fleet between Portland and the Thames, supplies of stone for the extension of Hampton Court were cut off. In the mounting tension the council decided on a round-up of suspected Jacobite sympathizers. Even poor old Pepys, who had earlier attempted to find a place in the new Parliament of March, and the Earl of Dartmouth, former commander-in-chief, were sent to the Tower 'on suspicion of being affected to King James'.

As the two fleets moved slowly up Channel, Torrington keeping carefully out of range and preventing the French from getting to the eastward of his fleet, Russell drafted a sharply worded order to fight. It was softened by the queen in council, and eventually issued in the following form: 'the consequence of his withdrawing to the Gunfleet would be so fatal, that she rather chooses he should, upon any advantage of wind, give battle to the enemy'. If he were to carry out his proposal of getting to the westward of the enemy fleet, he was on no account to lose sight of it, thus giving it no opportunity to make an attack on the shore or in the estuary.[6]

Countersigned by Nottingham, four copies of the queen's instructions were despatched to Torrington. His subordinate flag officers, including the Dutch, agreed that, though it would have been better to have been stronger, the queen's order must be obeyed. Tourville had likewise been left in no doubt about the importance of a successful engagement. On 27 June he received news of the victory of Luxembourg's army at Fleurus, and encouragement from Seignelay to fight as soon as possible.

At dawn on 30 June the allied fleet was seen off Beachy Head, bearing down towards him on the ebb tide with a wind from north-north-east. He formed his line on the starboard tack steering west of north, with 26 ships in each of his van and centre squadrons, and 25 in the rear. The allied line, elongated in order to cover the whole French fleet and to prevent doubling at either end, was formed with the 21 Dutch leading. The Dutch pressed home the attack and were soon in trouble, though Ashby as vice admiral of the red squadron tried to aid them, as Villette in the French van succeeded in tacking ahead of them and placing them between two fires. The rest of the red squadron came no closer than twice gunshot range, while Delaval took his greatly outnumbered blue squadron to within musket shot of d'Estrées at the rear of the French line.

The favourable wind did not hold. When it fell calm the allies attempted to tow their ships clear with their boats, and at five in the afternoon, after an engagement lasting eight hours, they anchored with all sails set as the ebb began to make. The French were slow to imitate them and drifted out of range, with one anchorless Dutch ship, the *Friesland*, in their midst. Torrington weighed later in the evening, when the flood set in, and resumed his retreat towards the Thames. He could not save the damaged ships, mainly Dutch, some of which were burnt on subsequent days along the shores of Rye Bay. Tourville lost no ships, though he had quite heavy casualties – about 400 killed and 500 wounded. From the Downs the beaten fleet, with a loss of 15 ships of all kinds, moved into the Thames estuary, taking up the buoys as it went. Its loss was very soon made good by a reinforcement of fresh Dutch ships, and of ten ships of 60–70 guns hired from the East India Company, but the consequences of the defeat were far-reaching.

Torrington was quite positive that, had he been left a free agent, he would have 'prevented any attempt upon the land, and secured the western ships, Killigrew and the merchantmen'. His first report to Carmarthen admitted the loss of one Dutch ship and many Dutch casualties, but asserted that the red squadron had prevented the loss of more of their lame ships. 'Had I undertaken this of my own hand, I should not well know what to say,' he concluded: 'but its being done by command will, I hope, free me from blame.'[7] Later naval historians have supported him. Richmond's summing up is the plainest: 'Between the responsibilities of the statesman and the commander there is a plain and distinct dividing line, and when one or other oversteps it into the other's province, the results are almost certain to be unfortunate.'[8] Mahan reached a similar conclusion, while Corbett approved of Torrington's tactics in the battle.

There have been many occasions in history when the best naval strategy has been to avoid action, or, if brought to action, to avert defeat. Torrington, his freedom of choice removed by the queen's positive order to engage, his advantage of the windward position lost by a piece of misfortune such as all naval and military commanders have to foresee, had done neither. It is a difficult posture to maintain without incurring charges of cowardice from those who do not have to fight, and sometimes equally from junior officers filled with the spirit of the offensive but ignorant of considerations of grand strategy. On this occasion Tourville could have done little harm had he been unable to engage.

In London there was near panic. Evelyn, never slow to cry woe, wrote: 'The whole nation now exceedingly alarmed by the French fleet braving our coast even to the very Thames mouth: our fleet commanded by debauched young men, and likewise inferior in force, giving way to the enemy, to our exceeding reproach.'[9] Fortunately the news was not all bad. Though the allies had lost a battle on the Continent at Fleurus, William had not gone to Ireland, as he put it, 'to let the grass grow under my feet'.[10] On 1 July, just over a fortnight after he landed and the day after the battle of Beachy Head, his army defeated James's at the Boyne.

William received an injury to a shoulder from a cannon ball on the day before the battle; Schomberg was killed in the action. Evelyn recorded on 13 July that there was much public rejoicing, but reverted to the perilous naval situation, with the French riding at present masters in 'our Channel', threatening to land.

William took a different and more realistic view; he did not fear a French landing because they had no troops embarked; he was principally concerned for the safety of his communications across the Irish sea. He had approved on 4 July the queen's order to Torrington to engage the enemy; by then both Beachy Head and the Boyne had been fought.

All the blame fell on Torrington. Even before the fleet left St Helen's, a suggestion had been made in council that a cabinet minister should share the command with him, a proposal which Queen Mary, whose inheritance of royal Stuart blood and of her Hyde grandfather's genius for administration was beginning to assert itself, wisely turned down. Devonshire later proposed that Torrington should be superseded, but the idea was rejected as too dangerous when he was actually in sight of the enemy. Monmouth, who had seen sea service as a young man between 1676 and 1679, and had commanded a Dutch squadron in the West Indies in 1687, had been pressing his suitability for the command. In the end he was sent with Russell, but they got no further than Canterbury; they were recalled to London on receipt of Torrington's acknowledgement of the order to engage. When the extent of the disaster became known, Pembroke and Devonshire were sent to the fleet at Deal, where they heard that a council of war of English officers was against the renewal of the fight.

Carmarthen was ready to jettison Torrington, and as early as 2 July was turning his thoughts, and those of the king, towards a successor, recommending Sir Richard Haddock as the best admiral. Haddock was a Tory member of Parliament, but he had no great achievements, and certainly no fighting successes, to his credit. Nottingham, forced by the pressure of work at this time to remain at his desk till three or four o'clock in the morning, was not so sure. Devonshire and Pembroke, he reported, could not find an officer in the fleet to criticize Torrington's conduct, though the same officers were supposed to have written very freely to their friends, blaming the earl severely. He also took a more optimistic view of the prospects. 'We can do little hurt to our enemies till we can get the fleet to sea again and strong enough to oppose them', he wrote for the king's eyes. Although there had been losses of ships, the rest would be repaired in a fortnight.[11]

The queen was chiefly upset by the comparatively heavy losses of the Dutch, accepting the widely held opinion that the English had left them to do the fighting alone. She wrote a personal letter to Evertsen, the

Dutch commander, and an abject apology to the States-General. The letter to Evertsen was at first 'with much ado' written in Dutch; but, on hearing that the admiral understood English, she recalled that version and wrote again in her own language. Nottingham told the English ambassador at the Hague to represent 'this wretched business' as well as he could. It was all due to Torrington.[12]

The government acted speedily to remove Torrington from the command. On 10 July the Sergeant-at-Arms was directed to take him into custody 'for high crimes and misdemeanours' and to deliver him to the Governor of the Tower, who was ordered to receive him and keep him in safe custody. There followed a considerable legal argument about jurisdiction and the nature of any trial, and the House of Lords later recorded that Torrington's committal by the Privy Council had been a breach of privilege.

Torrington was permitted to appear before the Lords in November. He spoke for about an hour. He blamed the defeat on the lack of naval preparations and intelligence. He had not been informed of the presence in the Channel of the French fleet, nor of its reinforcement by the Toulon squadron, before he saw them off the Isle of Wight. If the Secretary of State had not concealed from the queen the disparity in strength between the two fleets, she would not have sent him an order to fight, contrary to the opinion of a joint council of war. In the action itself he had done his best to save the fleet. The Dutch had engaged too soon, before they had reached the head of the French line. It was a fair defence, but it made little impression on the House.

It was not till the end of November that Delaval, as commander-in-chief of Their Majesties' Ships in the Thames and Medway, was ordered to enquire into, and try at court martial, the earl's conduct. The substance of the charge was that, having the command of the fleet, he had withdrawn and kept back, and had not done his utmost to damage the enemy and to assist his own and the Dutch ships in action and distress.[13] The court martial took place on 10 December; Torrington defended his conduct with spirit; a telling witness was John Benbow, the master-attendant at Deptford, a specialist in navigation and pilotage, who had served at Beachy Head as master of the fleet; the prosecution witnesses made a poor showing. The verdict of the court was unanimous: Torrington was acquitted.

His responsibility for the disaster had been prejudged by others besides the politicians at Court. Evelyn, visiting the Tower on other business soon after Torrington's committal, was directed by mistake to his quarters. He took the opportunity to record in his diary that the earl was there 'for his cowardice and not fighting the French fleet, which having beaten a squadron of Hollanders (while Torrington did nothing) did now ride masters at sea'.[14] The verdict made no difference; the admiral was dismissed from all his offices on 12 December. The English have never shown any mercy to unsuccessful admirals.

Torrington had been replaced long before, but not without a good deal of discussion and argument. Carmarthen had told the king shortly after the action that Russell would not accept the command, and that the choice lay between Haddock, Ashby, Shovell, Killigrew and Davies, unless His Majesty would employ Lord Grafton. The last suggestion was typical of seventeenth-century thought: rank was everything, and Grafton, as an illegitimate son of Charles II, was a duke. It accounts for the proposal, now seriously entertained by the council, that the command should be shared by three men, one to be a man of quality, with two seamen to assist him. Grafton, as it happened, was not lacking in sea experience. Sent to sea as a volunteer under Sir John Berry, he had twice assumed command of the 70-gun ship bearing his name, and had fought on board her at Beachy Head. He had earlier commanded a fleet sent to escort a new Queen of Portugal from Rotterdam to Lisbon and then to make peace with the Barbary states.

The queen rejected Monmouth's offers, which he had repeated, and told her husband that she heard that Shovell was the best officer of his age. Mary was at this time cheered by an offer to serve from her old friend Shrewsbury. Writing to Carmarthen on 12 July, he remarked that Russell was unwilling to take command; Pembroke was the obvious choice if a man of quality was required; but if Pembroke would not go, he offered himself. Though able to do little good, he would 'do as little hurt, which is all that can be expected from the best you can send'. He was sure that it was only seamen that could 'recover this disgrace'.[15]

Russell's advice was even firmer. He pointed out that 'not only the eye and expectation of all England, but all Europe, especially Holland, is upon this choice'; he did not think there was a man in England capable at this time to do it alone; he therefore recommended a commission of three on the lines already suggested; he thought Pembroke or Shrewsbury, but not Grafton, a suitable choice for the man of quality, and said nothing about the two admirals.[16] Pembroke, however, would not hear of such a thing, and the queen therefore thought it best to nominate two admirals, Haddock and Ashby, and to leave the selection of the third commissioner to the king.

When the Board of Admiralty waited on her at Kensington Palace on the evening of 22 July, she found that Pembroke and all the commissioners, except Russell and one other, were totally opposed to the notion of a commission and still recommended Russell alone. On 24 July the council summoned the Admiralty Commissioners and told them that it had decided to choose Killigrew, Ashby and Haddock as joint admirals. A furious argument ensued. Sir Thomas Lee, the elderly member of Parliament for Buckinghamshire, who had been the most earnest in presenting the Admiralty case at the previous meeting, maintained that the Crown could not appoint admirals of whom the Admiralty disapproved. The queen felt her anger rising. 'I perceive then,' she said, 'that the King has given away his own power and cannot make an admiral which the Admiralty do not like.'

'No, no more he can't,' Lee answered insolently.

Mary suppressed an angry rejoinder that in that case the king should give the Admiralty Commission to such as would not dispute with him.[17] The Commissioners were dismissed with instructions to prepare the warrant for the joint command of the three named admirals.

Talking the matter over with Russell next mornng, Mary was surprised to learn that the Admiralty objection was confined to the inclusion of Haddock for the simple reason that he was recommended by the Tory Nottingham. Russell again pressed for Shrewsbury as the third member. When Lee sent the Lord Chamberlain to apologize for his rudeness, the queen confessed that she had been very angry at what Sir Thomas had said, but now she was angrier on finding that it was passion, not reason, that made him speak thus. When Russell tried to excuse Lee, she said that were she in the king's place she would have dismissed him.

The Commissioners, in spite of reminders, were procrastinating over signing the commission, knowing presumably that all the arguments were being repeated to William in Ireland. Carmarthen complained to the king at the beginning of August that 'as faction is very natural amongst us, so it is as artificially and industriously improved as is possible, and always by the same hands'. He would not have the least doubt about the kingdom's ability to preserve itself if those 'who pretend to be your friends could but agree amongst themselves against the common enemy'.[18] He thought that the king's choice of Killigrew as the third member of the commission, when the queen left it to him, might raise difficulties because of clamour in the City about his tardy return from the Straits. Another obstacle was that Haddock was insisting that he ought to rank above the others, a point which, if conceded, would have made nonsense of the whole conception of a joint command. Carmarthen still favoured Russell as sole commander-in-chief as his first choice, with a commission of Pembroke, Killigrew and Ashby as his second.

On 5 August there was a full meeting of the Admiralty Board, and renewed instructions to issue the warrant were given. At last it was ready on 8 August, though it still lacked three signatures. One would prefer to think that those who abstained from signing did so because they recognized the evil of a joint command, but all the evidence points to party strife as the cause. When Carmarthen complained of it to William he had a sympathetic ear, for the king had already more than once marvelled at the English fondness for political faction; instead of fighting the enemy, they spent their time vilifying each other. So the command of the fleet was at last settled, and on 12 August its ships were assembled in the Downs.

The French had failed to exploit the successes they had obtained along the shores of Rye Bay. Tourville had gone no further towards the forelands, but had detached Relingue with five ships to join three from Dunkirk to watch the Pas de Calais. He also sent d'Amfreville with five of the line and two fireships to Irish waters. Seignelay's plan for the summer had envisaged the employment of new fast galleys built at Rochefort, and Tourville detached two ships to escort them across the Channel from la Hougue roads in Normandy. They were at sea by 16 July, but the night of the 21st proved rough, wet and windy. The galleys ran before the south-westerly blow into Torbay at midnight, and the rest of the French fleet anchored there at noon next day.

After a reconnaissance, Tourville selected Teignmouth as the objective for his attack. As an operation of war it was a futile expenditure of effort. The galleys and boats landed a total of 2,800 men under d'Estrées. A puny force of militia put up a token resistance, and after five hours ashore the French re-embarked, having burnt a few houses and some small coasting and fishing vessels, and captured three guns and seven prisoners. Like most warlike operations directed against the civil population rather than the armed forces, it only succeeded in strengthening the enemy's, that is the English, resolve to resist, and had no military effect whatever. When, later in the war, the English took to burning French coastal towns, Evelyn was one of those to be privately extremely critical of this manner of waging war. It was begun by the French, he complained, it was exceedingly ruinous, falling especially on the poorer people, and did not tend to shorten the war, but rather to exasperate and incite to revenge. There can be no doubt that he was right.

Tourville's fleet arrived back at Brest on 7 August with crews heavily depleted by sickness. It was time to lay up the great ships for the winter, but Nesmond was sent to Ireland with ten of the smaller ships. Both Louis and his Minister of Marine were furious at Tourville's failure to follow up his victory, and he was relieved of his command. Torrington, hearing of it, was able to remark grimly that it seemed odd for the French admiral to be dismissed for not destroying the English fleet, and for the English admiral to be dismissed for not allowing it to be destroyed.[19] It was particularly galling for Seignelay that the opportunity created by his reinforcement of the French fleet in the Channel had been squandered in this fashion. He had not recovered from the illness that had started at the end of the previous summer. Had he been fit, he would have embarked again with Tourville, and seen to it that a strong force of his smaller ships should penetrate to the Irish Sea in order to smash William's communications. This was the purpose for which the allied fleet had been defeated: the object was to secure Ireland for James as a prelude to his restoration to the thrones of England and Scotland. The destruction of an insignificant fishing port could not possibly exert any influence towards this end.

The English, in contrast to their opponents, showed remarkable resilience. They not only sustained the army in Ireland with supplies from Chester and Bristol, but put in hand an offensive operation to hasten the total conquest of the island. In the initial confusion after the defeat off Beachy Head, William had responded to Carmarthen's pleadings by marching towards the sea with five regiments. But on hearing that the French fleet had left the English coast, he resumed his advance on Limerick.

James had meanwhile moved first to Dublin, where urgent letters from his queen at St Germains caused Tyrconnel to advise him to return to France. James continued south to Waterford, going thence by sea to Kinsale, finally embarking in a French frigate for passage back to Brest. Ireland was left in the charge of Tyrconnel, with powers to make peace or continue the war. Before he left Ireland James received a letter from the French king, flushed with the victory at Fleurus, offering to land him in England at the head of an army of 30,000 men. But, back in France, he found that Louis was unable to go forward with the project, which was opposed by both his ministers of war and of marine. James drew a scrap of comfort from a report that his daughter Mary had said that she was glad he had not lost his life in Ireland.

William, after an unsuccessful assault on Limerick on 27 August, raised the siege, put Ginkel in command of the army, and headed for England, reaching Hampton Court on 10 September. In spite of the defeat of the fleet, he had every reason to be proud of the way his wife had managed affairs in his absence, and to be satisfied that he would be able to resume his close attention to political and military affairs on the Continent.

Marlborough had meanwhile proposed an attack on Cork and Kinsale; Waterford had already fallen without a shot in July. Ministers, except Nottingham, were against the new offensive, but the king approved. As a political decision it was akin to the despatch of troops and tanks to Egypt after the evacuation at Dunkirk in 1940. Marlborough's land force consisted of 5,000 English and 4,000 Danes under the Duke of Württemberg. It embarked at Portsmouth at the end of August, but the convoy under the joint admirals could not sail before 17 September, and reached southern Ireland on the 21st. Cork was quickly taken, followed by Kinsale; Marlborough added to his growing military reputation, and was able to leave Ireland on board the *Lennox* on 18 October, and to be back at Deal before the end of the month. Tyrconnel had withdrawn the French

troops to Galway, and had sailed for France on 12 September, leaving
Berwick in command of the army, another example of the fashion for
rewarding rank rather than experience. Berwick marched towards Cork,
but was too late to intervene.

The House of Commons was in a robust mood in the autumn of 1690.
William opened Parliament on 2 October, and it voted a Royal Navy of
28,000 men, and over half a million pounds expressly for building 27 new
warships. In November it imposed new or increased taxes on ale,
liquors, East Indies goods, wrought silks, wine, vinegar and tobacco.

Trade had of course been disrupted by the French temporary command of the Channel in the summer of 1690, but again the news was not
all gloomy. Killigrew, his ships foul after their long period in commission, reached Plymouth on 7 July with the trade from Cadiz. Other safe
arrivals increased the number of sail there to 300 by early August, when
news of the French fleet's return to Brest released them, and they came
safely to the Thames by the end of the month. Delaval's squadron in the
Channel intercepted a Swedish convoy bound for France with naval
stores, and captured seven of them. Another squadron under Sir Francis
Wheeler intercepted a French man-of-war carrying James's despatches
from Ireland, then a convoy of 26 sail on their way from France to Ireland
with stores, provisions and ammunition. Convoys were sailed in
December for Spain, Portugal, the West Indies and Virginia. Aylmer,
who had commanded the *Royal Catherine* in Delaval's blue squadron at
Beachy Head, was sent to the Straits with 14 ships to confirm peace with
the Barbary corsairs, and to bring home the Smyrna trade, which had
arrived safely in the Levant in October.

An event had already taken place that was to alter the whole basis of
allied trade protection. What appeared a serious blow to France's naval
administration fell when Seignelay died at Versailles in Tourville's presence in October. Pontchartrain, his successor, though widely thought to
be no more than a courtier with a taste for poetry, a somewhat indolent
man aged 47, ushered in an entirely new maritime strategy for France.
The new minister regarded the king's navy as an unnecessary expense
while it spent its time seeking or avoiding the allied fleet. His first
proposal was to disband the king's navy altogether; the coasts of France
could be protected more economically and more effectively by 30,000
militia. Fortunately Louis took a second opinion: it was from Bonrepaus,
the Intendant-General, who pointed out in the following summer that
the navy's task was to protect not only the coasts, but the commerce and
troop transports of France.

Pontchartrain's second thoughts were more sensible. If privateers
could pay for themselves by operating against allied trade, he argued,
why could not the fleet do likewise? Thus began the *guerre de course*, the
age of the corsair, a war directed against the trade by which England and

Holland lived, and therefore a war to which both were particularly vulnerable. Though England learned, after some sharp lessons, how to counter it, the lessons were promptly forgotten, and had to be re-learned at great cost over and over again in the eighteenth and again in the twentieth century.

The final act of naval importance for the year was the appointment of Edward Russell in sole command of the fleet for the coming summer. Sanity of principle had returned in the reversion to a single commander, but there remained something of a question mark over the suitability of this outspoken, political admiral to a command he had hitherto steadfastly refused to accept. Mary had found him a useful adviser; of all her Council she had found him the easiest to talk to and the soundest in his advice. Burnet, who had come to know him well during the planning and in the early days of the revolution, gave him a good character, full of the most excellent principles. On the other hand a naval subordinate called him 'excessively proud and haughty; difficult to be pleased unless flattered and implacable if offended'.[20] This assessment, if correct, would not necessarily make him unsuitable for the command in chief. Charnock's near-contemporary naval biography allows him a natural affability which, added to his rank as a duke's nephew, 'had gained him an ascendancy over the hearts of naval people'.[21] Macaulay, who never disguises his partiality, refers to Russell's irritable and imperious nature, and calls him a false, arrogant, and wayward politician. A modern writer uses the adjectives coarse-minded, outspoken, ignorant and brutal.[22]

It is difficult to reach a just conclusion on his showing up to this time, but his lively correspondence, much of which survives, shows him possessed of a particularly clear mind on the correct employment of naval force as an instrument of national policy. It has been suggested that he suffered from pique when the command for 1690 went to Torrington instead of to himself. But to argue from this that, by advising the queen to order Torrington to fight, he deliberately set out to accomplish the earl's ruin, is to suggest a lack of patriotism totally out of keeping with his character. He was now to command the allied fleet for the two critical years of 1691 and 1692.

Chapter 4

Map 1. Western Europe

Resurgence

William was anxious to visit Holland as soon as possible, and he left London again early in the new year of 1691. He took Nottingham with him, and appointed Sidney, who had been with him in Ireland, as the second secretary of state. He was discovering a shortage of talent for his administration, but he thought that Sidney would do until he could find someone better.

The king had a long and eventually perilous crossing. He sailed on 18 January from Gravesend in the yacht *Mary*, and was met by Rooke from the Downs with his escort in Margate roads. It was some time before they were able to sail, and then thick weather prevented them from making the land. William, accompanied by Devonshire and Zuylestein, now a naturalized Englishman, completed the journey in an open boat for 16 hours in freezing fog before landing in his native country on 21 January. His impatience is understandable, but there is no record of the sentiments of the escort commander about the king's impetuosity in such weather conditions.

William's object was to hold a conference at the Hague in order to strengthen the Continental alliance and to confirm his leadership of it after his absence in England and Ireland. He was not allowed to forget naval affairs. He had hardly left London before Carmarthen was writing to him to ask him to use his influence 'on that side of the water' to improve the provision of intelligence on the French ports of Brest, St Malo and Dunkirk. The French ships at the latter port were a particular menace, and the English were determined to prevent them from joining the main fleet at Brest. They did not sail on the spring tide of 18 February, and by the end of the month the English already had some lighter ships in the Downs to watch for them should they come out on the next springs on 4 March. Delaval was ordered to shift his flag from the *Royal Sovereign* to a 3rd-rate and to cruise off Dunkirk with eight or ten ships, while the usual preparations of the main fleet went forward in the Thames and Medway.

These measures were effective in preventing the French ships in Dunkirk from getting to the westward, for the French feared that they would be picked off one by one as they cleared the shoals. Bart and Forbin, both of whom had fought at Beachy Head, and had afterwards joined Relingue's squadron in the narrow seas, therefore conceived the idea that small ships might slip out by night and prey on allied commerce in the North Sea. The project was approved by the new Minister of Marine, and in mid-July the pair of them sailed in company, and were successfully clear of the allied blockading squadron by daybreak. Bart chose a dark and rainy night at spring tides with a south-easterly wind. Altogether 20 sail came out of Dunkirk – seven warships with two fireships, seven or eight privateers, and the rest merchantmen, two of which were taken by the allied squadron under the Dutch captain Toll.

Bart and Forbin quickly captured three ships bound for north Russian ports with a single escort, and sent their prizes into Bergen. Then they burned a fleet of herring busses, and took its Dutch escort. Prisoners were landed on the English coast, and in Northumberland an attack was made on the castle of a known Roman Catholic in order to remind him of his duty. But the ill-assorted pair fell out before the end of the cruise, which achieved its object of capturing or destroying many allied merchant vessels, and of spreading alarm in the seaports of the east coasts of England and Scotland. Nottingham told Russell before the end of July that eight enemy privateers were off our northern coasts and had landed in Northumberland, and in early August Bart was reported off the Orkneys.

There was one English success when Aylmer in the *Monk* took a Dunkirker off Scarborough in September. He managed to locate Bart's squadron cleaning their ships in Bergen, and kept the men of his own small force on short allowance of provisions in order to remain in the offing. The weather, as so often, dictated otherwise, forcing Aylmer back to the Downs by 5 October. Bart sailed three weeks later for Dunkirk.

Though some of Russell's fleet were at the buoy of the Nore before the end of March, and Prince George of Denmark inspected a representative ship of each rate there on the 15th, there were the usual delays in getting the fleet manned, armed, rigged and provisioned for sea. Some ships were still not ready when the king returned with Devonshire from Holland on 22 April, bringing 20 Dutch ships with him, passing through the English fleet amid the smoke of gun salutes. Louis, angry at the political success of William's conference at the Hague, had opened the land campaign sooner than was customary, and had captured the frontier fortress of Mons early in April. Berwick had left the Irish troops to Sarsfield, and was with the French army at this time. William had no intention of staying long in England; he was gone again on 1 May, after bringing the steady and talented Godolphin and the dull and almost useless Prince George of Denmark on to the Council in place of Marlborough and Monmouth. On this occasion he took Sidney with him, and left Nottingham at Whitehall. Rooke again took command of the escort.

In April Haddock had come down to the fleet from London, and had paid the companies of all ships their bounty and pay up to the previous 1 October. They sailed for the Downs in the middle of May, and by the end of the month a fine array had assembled. Russell's flag flew in the *Britannia*, a 1st-rate built at Chatham by Phineas Pett, one of a celebrated family of naval architects, in 1682. She mounted 100 guns, and carried a complement of 710 men. In Russell's red squadron Ashby was vice admiral in the *Victory*, Rooke the rear admiral on board the *Neptune*. The blue squadron was commanded by Killigrew in the *Duke*, with Delaval returned from cruising off Dunkirk and his vice admiral's flag back in the *Royal Sovereign*, and Shovell's rear admiral's flag in the *London*. The Dutch as usual supplied the white squadron. The whole fleet sailed on 9 June, in good weather but mainly westerly winds. On the third day out the wind veered to north-east, and the fleet was able to spread in line abreast, covering a nine-mile front as it swept down Channel. Off Plymouth the wind came back to its prevailing south-westerly direction with drizzle, so Russell put into Torbay.

The French were already at sea. Tourville had been reinstated, and had 75 of the line and 20 fireships with him. Six ships from Dunkirk had managed to elude the allies and to reach Brest with two prizes, an English ship of 54 guns and an Ostender of 44. Tourville's orders were to keep the Channel open so as to transport help to Ireland and to hinder the enemy from doing likewise. He was also instructed to intercept trade, particularly the valuable homeward Smyrna convoy, and told that Louis did not desire him to attack the allied fleet.

As in the previous year the French had successfully run reinforcements across to Galway in April, before the allies could come so far west. Mary blamed Russell's delays for this discouragement to William's friends in Ireland, but the fleet could not be strong everywhere. The presence of enemy ships in Dunkirk presented a more immediate threat to the king on passage to and from Holland, and to London's trade. The squadron based on the Downs had to take precedence over any western fleet.

Although Russell was subsequently severely criticized for not bringing the French to action during the summer of 1691, all the evidence tends to show that he did his best to do so. His critics failed to appreciate how easily two fleets, even large ones, can avoid meeting in an area as vast as the south-western approaches to the British Isles, particularly if one side is intent, as the French were, on avoiding contact. The critics had the evidence of the safe arrival of the inward Smyrna convoy, which the French were attempting to find, but they chose to ignore it. Before he left the Downs Russell declared: 'though I am very far from loving fighting 'twas for that purpose only I undertook this campaign'.[1] He and Nottingham agreed that, if the French fleet would not fight, there was no point in burning a French town, as Teignmouth had been burnt.

There is another letter of Russell's, written to the king from the *Britannia* on 10 May, that shows that he fully expected action. 'Since the accidents of war may possibly put it out of my power of having the honour to see Your Majesty again', he began, and went on, in a passage typifying the power of seventeenth-century patronage, to plead for his brother, who had done his duty in Ireland but could not live on the emoluments of a lieutenant-colonel of horse. Russell, in spite of the £3,000 he drew from the Crown and his own little fortune, had considerable debts as a result, he alleged, of his expensive voyages, and could not help his brother. A whole year had passed since his return from escorting the Queen of Spain; this voyage may well have proved expensive in entertainment.

There is perhaps here a clue to Russell's reluctance to accept the command-in-chief; apart from his preference for the political life, he was financially better off ashore. Another reason for his wishing to avoid prolonged absence at sea almost certainly lay in his intention to marry, in this year of 1691, his cousin Lady Margaret Russell, a daughter of the Earl of Bedford.

From Torbay the allied fleet cast across to Ushant for news of Tourville. They obtained none, but ascertained that the Smyrna fleet, escorted by the handsome Irishman Matthew Aylmer, had reached Kinsale in safety. According to Evelyn, who was no doubt reporting the gossip of the London merchants, the ships in convoy narrowly escaped the French, and were 'put to extraordinary suffering by foul weather carrying them far to the west, which was, by God's providence, the cause of their safety'.[2] The use of the southern Irish ports, so recently captured, was already proving invaluable.

Russell sailed there, and off Kinsale, in 'thick hurry durry weather' as the log of the *Defiance* has it, received his first positive intelligence of the French fleet when the *Adventure* joined him, with topgallant sails loosed and flying in the wind to denote an enemy sighting, to report it 75 miles to the southward. A cast in that direction brought no contact, and the fleet came back to Ireland to see the convoy safely past the Scillies. In accordance with the practice of the time some men from these merchant vessels, so nearly home from a long voyage, were heartlessly pressed to make up numbers in the warships. Russell detached three English and two Dutch ships to watch the approaches to Limerick, and took the rest of the fleet with the convoy. Then he took station again off Ushant.

He was already apprehensive about the reported censure in London of the fleet's alleged inactivity, and complained to Nottingham of its injustice. He had taken all the care he could to ensure that the convoy from the Mediterranean should run no hazard. In addition to covering its passage from Ireland with the whole fleet, he had sent the *James* galley ahead to Plymouth for any information about enemy activity on its route. He hit the nail exactly on the head when he wrote that he was 'very much of opinion that their [the French] fleet lies in the sea the better to avoid us, it being pretty difficult to find their rendezvous'. A few days later he enquired plaintively whether, if he were so unhappy as not to meet the enemy, 'the Queen would have a Teignmouth burnt on the coast of France, or how Her Majesty would have the fleet proceed'.[3]

Arrived off Ushant, Russell heard from Plymouth that the outward West Indies convoy, escorted by the *Mary Rose* and *Constant Warwick*, had fallen in with the French fleet; both warships and eight or nine merchant vessels had been taken. Russell expressed his amazement that the convoy had been allowed to sail when it was known that the enemy fleet was at sea hoping to intercept the homeward trade, and therefore in a good position to catch any outward-bound shipping. Russell said he did not know a better man than Shovell; after a council of war he detached him in the frigate *Plymouth*, with 16 of the smaller English and Dutch ships, to take a closer look at Brest. After capturing a French frigate with refugees from Ireland, leaving Russell with 'two damn'd Irish friars and three fair lady passengers to Brest' to look after, Shovell showed French colours, and thus contrived to get close to a French convoy in the approaches. He took a few of them, all small, and the *Bridget* galley drove one ashore and burned her. More important, he gained definite intelligence of Tourville, who was said to be cruising 150 miles west-south-west of Ushant.

After another council of war, Russell spread the fleet in line abreast at wide intervals so that it covered a front of over 30 miles, and swept westward in search of the French fleet. The opposing scouts made contact, but Tourville merely withdrew further into the broad expanse of the Atlantic; he had 10 to 15 ships fewer than the allies and had no intention of being brought to action. By remaining in the position of the French rendezvous and showing French flags, Russell was able to take an auxiliary with water and another with fresh provisions, but he could not hold this position indefinitely. A volunteer on board Delaval's flagship, the *Royal Sovereign*, remarked in his journal that she had never before been so far from home.[4] As July advanced there was the usual anxiety about keeping the 1st- and 2nd-rates at sea later than mid-August. The wind remaining westerly, a council of war decided to return to the Channel, and Ushant was in sight again on 1 August. There were a dozen or so French ships to windward next day, but they slipped past in the night to reach harbour unmolested. Russell was disappointed at his failure to meet and fight the enemy. 'But this will always be the case', he remarked philosophically. 'When you are weak, they will come out and beat you; when strong, avoid you, which is to be done with great ease.'[5]

The French, in fact, were exercising the policy of keeping their 'fleet in being'. Tourville called it his *campagne du large*, and has been credited with the invention of an original strategy. It was his decided opinion that, once the main fleets came in sight of each other in open waters, the weaker could not avoid being brought to action except by abandoning its slowest ships. Events were to show France in the following year, as the allies had been taught in 1690, the disastrous consequences of political interference with the policy of keeping a 'fleet in being' when it would have been correct to apply it. Russell thought that it was not enough for the allies to have a strong fleet at sea in the Channel, but he left his ideas on 'some other project' for later discussion in London.

The *Hope* and the *Resolution* took small prizes on 3 and 5 August, but Russell had many men sick with scurvy; both the English and the Dutch ships were short of beer and water. The fleet met the victuallers off the Lizard on 10 August and proceeded to Torbay. Orders had been sent from Whitehall that it should go to Kinsale for refreshment; the Government did not want Ireland left open to reinforcement from France during the concluding phases of the land campaign. Like Tourville before him, Russell failed to appreciate the importance of interrupting the sea communications of an army committed to fight overseas. There can be no doubt that his correct strategic base at this time lay in Ireland. Torbay lay too far to the eastward; more important, it lay too far leeward in the prevailing winds. Nottingham's letter of 29 July, with the queen's instructions to refresh at Kinsale, did not reach Russell till he had reached Torbay, after the *James* galley had searched fruitlessly for him off Ushant. The commander-in-chief thought that Her Majesty had not been well advised to order the fleet to Kinsale, where ships, he alleged, must ride exposed to the weather. This sounds like a piece of special pleading: the southern Irish ports owed their existence to their ability to give shelter, though Russell's view, that those of the first two rates could not lie there in safety, must be respected.

On the same day, 11 August, Nottingham was sending off copies of an earlier letter and instructions, summarizing the latter as meaning firstly that the fleet should fight the French if an opportunity occurred, secondly that it should secure the safe return of the trade from America, and thirdly that it should protect the transport of troops from Ireland. Nottingham added some intelligence that 14 French ships had reached Limerick, and that 30 more were expected there to carry troops from Ireland to France.

It was a perplexed and querulous admiral who sat down after midnight to write a reply. He confessed himself at a loss how to carry out the queen's instructions, which gave him three unrelated tasks, each of which required the fleet to be in a different place. He represented strongly that the fleet ought not to be in the ocean at all at this time of year, but that the protection of the inward trade must mean it lying in the Soundings, that is some 90 miles to the south-westward of the Isles of

Scilly. He knew nothing of any troop movements from Ireland, and again stressed that no harbour on the south coast of Ireland was safe for the great ships. Finally he detected a note of censure in the repeated order to fight the French. He had done his best, he told Nottingham, and all his decisions had been confirmed, without a dissenting voice, by the English and Dutch flag officers in company. He had been distressed to hear that his reputation, which he had always endeavoured to preserve, had been tossed about like a tennis ball.

The truth was that Russell was in the wrong place. Had he taken his fleet to the south of Ireland, he would have been well placed to protect the inward trade. Indeed 72 ships from Virginia, with two escorts, reached Kinsale on 17 August to await stronger convoy up the Channel, while 30 or 40 more went on to Bristol. By early September the Barbados convoy had likewise arrived at Kinsale, representing with the earlier arrivals at least £300,000 in customs dues on unloading in the Thames, revenue earnestly wanted by the Crown. But the onset of autumn storms from the south-west made it impossible, in spite of reiterated orders, to send more escorts to Ireland. There would have been no problem had the fleet been there. Again, there was but one sure way of bringing the French fleet, or a part of it, to action: it was to place the fleet where it could effectively prevent further reinforcements or supplies from reaching Limerick. Repeated intelligence of such an intention on the part of the enemy continued to reach Whitehall, and to be passed on to Russell. The admiral himself kept reminding Nottingham of the risks run by leaving a small squadron in the Shannon, where it might easily be overpowered. The best insurance against such a happening would have been the presence of the main fleet in Irish waters.

But now it was at Torbay, and a council of war on 19 August decided that there was no point in staying at sea after the end of the month, that there should be an absolute ban on remaining out after 10 September, and that the best general rendezvous for orders was Spithead. If these dates appear early, it should be remembered that they are all taken from the old style calendar, and that ten days must be added to arrive at new style, and thus modern, equivalents. Equinoctial gales were much feared, and it was unreasonable to risk the great ships later than what we should call 20 September.

The fleet had replenished, and Russell had complimented the victuallers on the way they had performed their duties, but he lingered in harbour, writing almost daily for clear sailing orders from the Admiralty. For three days the wind was easterly, but on 21 August it came round to west once more. It was not till the 25th that the Admiralty replied. Their Lordships said, in effect, that orders had been issued as long ago as the 11th, an imputation vigorously refuted by Russell as he complained to the Secretary of State that matters of such consequence should not be open to double interpretation. It was now known that Tourville's fleet had entered Camaret roads, at the entrance to Brest, on 6 August, just as Russell's sails had disappeared northward. Nottingham, who had intelligence that the French were pressing men for their fleet, reverted to the desirability of an attack on the enemy in Camaret Bay, if such an attack could be contrived without too much hazard. A council of war at Torbay on 25 August thought an attack inadvisable, but Russell sailed at last on the 28th with a final reflection that it would have been better if he and the Lords of the Admiralty had understood one another sooner.

The fleet made Ushant on the morning of 31 August, and stood in till the evening. Again next morning they approached within nine miles of the mainland without sighting a single sail. Then the bad weather, which Russell had so much feared, set in with a hard gale from south-south-east towards midnight on 2 September. Many ships lost their longboats, and the frigate *Plymouth* her main topmast. Next morning the fleet bore away for shelter on the English coast. Russell's red squadron drove before the gale into Plymouth, but the *Harwich* grounded under Mount Edgcumbe, was overset, and became a total loss, while the *Coronation*, a 2nd-rate of 90 guns, turned over with a very heavy loss of life while veering cable after anchoring. Commanded by Charles Skelton, she had been Delaval's flagship at Beachy Head in the previous year. Two other ships took the ground aft, but were successfully refloated.

Delaval's blue squadron tried to make Falmouth, but were unable to weather Dodman Point, and therefore entered Plymouth also. The Dutch decided to tack and stand off the land. On the whole it was safer if less comfortable, though one Dutch ship lost all her masts and had to be towed to Spithead by the *Berwick*.

There was as usual a good deal of uninformed criticism of the fleet's losses, coupled with its failure to fight the enemy. It was not long before a scurrilous song complained that the ships had sailed in May and returned in September 'with the loss of some ships, but in battle none slain'. We can contrast this with a contemporary seaman's view. The captain of the *Grafton* recorded that the damage was 'not very significant in consideration of the storm that happened'.[6] The real fault lay with the administration in sending the fleet to sea for no real purpose and against the advice of its admiral. Carmarthen tended to minimize the losses when he reported to the king; he was careful to point out that all the contents of the *Harwich* had been saved, and her timbers could be used again for a new ship.

The song went on to assert that the fleet had a total of 6,078 guns, but 'it had been the same thing had they left 'em ashore'. All this must have been galling to Russell, who had a notoriously low boiling point in matters of personal criticism, and never acquired the hard skin of the politician. Worse still, the song made slanderous allegations that Lady Margaret Russell, 'to whom he had promised his heart and his hand', had in her youth been 'otherwise mann'd'.[7]

The song can only have come to Russell's notice later on, but he was already beside himself with rage and frustration. He had taken care throughout the summer to preserve the fleet so that there would be an inconsiderable charge for refitting it for the following year. Before this latest sortie, he pointed out, no ship required more than cleaning and caulking – their hulls, masts, sails and cordage were all intact. Why employ an admiral to command the fleet, he asked plaintively, and pay no attention to his opinion, supported as it had been by all his junior flag officers?

The whole fleet re-assembled at Spithead, but only to disperse for the winter. The English 1st- and 2nd-rates made for the Thames to be laid up. One of them, the *Vanguard*, ran aground on the Goodwins, was refloated in a leaking condition, and beached near Sandwich; by mid-September she was safe in the Downs again. Most of the Dutch returned to Holland. Russell himself, who had not set a foot ashore for three and a half months, went to London, leaving Delaval with the smaller ships to cruise to the westward, his flag in the *Berwick*.

The chief concern in London was the final reduction of Limerick. In July there had been good news from Ireland. First there was a success at Athlone, followed by a decisive victory at Aughrim, a few miles nearer Galway. Carmarthen, clear-sighted as usual, at once started considering the next year's employment for the army that would shortly be released. Parliament, he told the king, would grumble if they were sent to reinforce the allied armies in Flanders, but it would approve a direct attack on France. After consulting some of the Huguenot officers, he suggested that 10,000 foot and 2,500 horse with an artillery train would be sufficient to lay waste Normandy. They could sail direct from Galway. He added another argument for landing in France: by that means the French fleet might be drawn into battle.

All this was long-term planning; the campaign was not yet over. Towards the end of August Ginkel was emphasizing the importance of preventing the relief of Limerick by French ships. Delaval attempted to carry out his orders throughout the autumn, but was continually driven back by south-westerly gales. He was told not to recall the ships in the Shannon without Ginkel's consent. Limerick at last surrendered on 3 October; the news reached London on the 10th. Ginkel gave generous terms: any of the defeated army who wished to go to France might do so; the rest might transfer to William's army or go home. His negotiation of the surrender was just in time: only two days later a French relieving force of 18 ships arrived with stores and ammunition. The French and Irish stuck to the terms of the surrender instrument; the fleet returned to

France, but several Irish regiments went with it; other Irish regiments marched to Cork for passage in English transports.

Honours, or at least titles, showered on the victors: Ginkel became Earl of Athlone; the younger Schomberg, who had distinguished himself as general of horse after his father the duke's death at the Boyne, and had now taken on English nationality, was made Duke of Leinster, with his father's Order of the Garter and £3,000 a year; Ruvigny, who took over command of the Huguenot cavalry from Schomberg, became Viscount Galway. On James's side, Tyrconnel had died in Limerick; Sarsfield, created Earl of Lucan by James, went to France.

William had another idea for the employment of the winter squadron. He expected the Spanish *flota* from the Caribbean to reach Cadiz about the middle of October, bringing cargo to the value of 40,000 crowns; about half of this would be in English and Dutch bottoms, and would require onward convoy. He suggested a squadron of 15 English and nine Dutch for this duty. Delaval pleaded for the command, pointing out to Nottingham the advantages received by other officers. He was at Torbay on 14 October, but his Dutch contingent under Callenburg was still at Spithead, whence it sailed six days later to join him. The squadron did eventually get away towards Ireland, but by 11 November it had been forced back again by a storm; Delaval reported that the Dutch ships were in no condition to continue, and he virtually gave up any further attempt to carry out his orders.

The fleet's long cruise had not been without gain. Russell had issued revised fighting instructions, and had been given a great opportunity to establish an understanding with his flag officers and captains. No fleet can fight successfully without this intangible asset, and Russell was to be given no time to foster it in the following year before the fleets were locked in combat. Tourville, driven back to harbour by sickness and lack of victuals after 50 days at sea, had been given a similar opportunity to drill his ships; his sole success had been the capture of the West Indies convoy and its escort three days out from Falmouth.

This convoy should not have been lost. It should have been sailed under the cover of the whole fleet instead of being sent out with a weak escort. Such an employment of the fleet would have been more likely to bring on the desired action than its constant cruising in the western approaches. The blame for this lapse lies with the administration rather than with the commander-in-chief, and the reason for it lies partly in the uncertain dividing line between the responsibilities of the Privy Council and the Admiralty, but mainly in the failure to grasp the fact that convoys needed an escort capable of fighting off the most powerful force to threaten their safe passage. If this threat came from the enemy battle fleet, then the allied fleet must cover the convoy until clear of danger. Allocation of a number of ships to trade protection under Admiralty

control, and of the rest to a Grand Fleet controlled more by the Privy
Council than by the Admiralty, was a policy that did not work. Russell
himself exhibited a very clear understanding of the purpose of a battle
fleet. 'If there be a prospect of doing service,' he wrote early in September, after wind and weather had driven him back to harbour, 'your
fleet ought to be ventured. 'Tis for that purpose they were built, and not
to be looked on or talked of; but unless there be such hopes, the less they
are hazarded . . . the better.'[8]

The new fighting instructions have been credited to Torrington. Sir
Julian Corbett has said of them: 'No one document probably possesses so
much for the history of naval tactics as the instructions issued by Admiral
Russell in 1691.' They were a natural development from those issued in
1673 by James when Duke of York and Lord High Admiral, and they
were the foundation on which all subsequent fighting instructions
issued in the age of sail were built. They depended on simple single-flag
or two-flag signals hoisted in different positions – red, white or blue
flags, or the union flag, hoisted at the fore topmast head, the main
topmast head or at the mizzen peak. There were also general instructions
that needed no signal, such as number 19, which directed each captain to
take care not to fire 'till he is sure that he can reach the enemy upon a
point-blank'; and number 23, which said that if any ship were disabled
the ship ahead was to 'take her a-tow', but they were not to leave the line
until the flag officer had been informed and his directions had been
received.[9]

The line of battle was the fighting formation, but the instructions
allowed flexibility in forming it if some ships were to windward or to
leeward of the admiral. It was possible for the admiral to direct the blue
or white squadron to tack and endeavour to gain the wind of the enemy,
to order a general chase or a single squadron to chase, or to tell ships at
anchor to cut or slip their cables. The order to engage the enemy was the
hoisting of a red flag at the fore topmast head. In contemporary accounts
it is sometimes referred to as 'putting out the bloody flag' or 'showing the
flag of defiance'. It was quite usual for messages with fresh orders to
individual ships, or with reports from them, to be despatched by boat,
even when in action, and frigates could be used to repeat general signals
which intervening ships and the smoke of powder might obscure, just as
Jellicoe used repeating ships at Jutland 225 years later.

The admiral had no staff to advise him or with whom to discuss plans
beyond a 'first captain', carried in addition to the captain of the fleet
flagship, and a senior specialist in navigation and pilotage serving as
master of the fleet. As will have been seen from the account of the
campaign, it was customary for all policy decisions to be confirmed by a
council of war. It was usually a relatively simple matter in good weather
conditions, whether at sea or in harbour, to summon flag officers on

board the fleet flagship for the purpose. After the disaster of the previous year it was necessary to treat the Dutch with special care; Russell was the right man to restore their confidence in English leadership. Thus the summer campaign of 1691 allowed Russell to exercise his squadrons in company for many days on end, so that by the end of it he had a well-tempered weapon under his hand.

Granted that Russell was not a great man, nor even a great admiral, it is surely an exaggeration to write, as Laughton did in 1893, of his 'blundering incapacity', and to assert that he had 'no conception of tactics, no knowledge or experience of the art of handling a fleet'.[10]

In London men could see only that merchant shipping had been lost, and that the main fleets had not met to dispute the mastery of the Channel. Thus Evelyn on 11 July: 'No news where either ours or the French fleets are, whilst our merchants here in extreme apprehension for their Smyrna fleet.' But eight days later he could record that the Smyrna fleet had arrived safe in Kinsale and that there was great rejoicing in London.[11] Subsequently he lamented the losses inflicted by privateers from Dunkirk, in spite of our watch on the port, and noted the loss to the French of 'our merchants of Russia's ships' and 'our Barbados fleet'.

Allied privateers were as active as those of the enemy: those of Zeeland, based on Flushing and Middelburg, numbered over 30; there were also 20 English, fewer in this year than before or afterwards. Although, soon after the declaration of war in 1689, the Crown had drawn up a commission to the Lords of the Admiralty to issue letters of marque against France, the English authorities did not care for privateering; by offering the incentive of gain to seamen it tended to interfere with naval manning. But it was a good way to disrupt French trade; during the whole period covered by this study, from 1689 to 1693, French losses in prize were about the same as the combined English and Dutch losses, making France proportionately the heaviest loser of the three.[12] The difference between the antagonists was that, while France did not depend on overseas trade, neither England nor Holland could survive without it. Dunkirk, behind the Flanders shoals, was ideally placed as a base for privateers. All the richest cargoes, to and from the Thames, the Netherlands and the Hanseatic ports, passed close by. The chops of the Channel provided another good hunting ground for privateers based on St Malo, Brest and Nantes, whether French or commissioned by James.

Another positive gain made during the summer campaign of 1691 was the marked improvement in the standard of victualling. New commissioners had been appointed in the winter of 1689–90, after the dreadful sickness and mortality in Torrington's fleet; the results of their stewardship showed in the quality of the food and drink distributed to Russell's ships, and in the consequently improved health record.

No great achievements stood to the credit of the allied armies on the

Continent, but the frontier barrier held. William, on board the yacht *Mary* escorted by Shovell, reached Margate in 24 hours from Holland on 19 October. His coach upset on Shooter's Hill as it descended from Blackheath, but he escaped injury. Three days later he opened Parliament, and in November the Commons voted over £1½ million for the Royal Navy. They called Russell to the bar of the House. He could have defended himself in professional terms but, being a Whig and a party man, chose to do so by attacking the administration, particularly Nottingham, the Tory Secretary of State, thus laying the seeds of much trouble to come. It was widely believed that he had made no effort to find the French fleet. Evelyn was only repeating the popular opinion when he wrote: 'our fleet come in to lay up the great ships, nothing done at sea, pretending that we cannot meet with the French'. He blamed the great losses of merchant vessels on 'negligence, and unskilful men governing both fleet and Navy'.[13] Others, always ready to smell treachery, attributed the fleet's failure to Jacobite leanings on the part of the commander-in-chief.

There was of course a good deal of intercourse by letter and by personal messenger between England and the Court at St Germains. At the time of Beachy Head, Mary was made aware of a leakage of information from her council by means of letters with secret writing. One of her objects in sending Monmouth with Russell to join the fleet at Dover was to confirm her suspicions that Monmouth was the author. It will be remembered that the two councillors were stopped at Canterbury, but the secret correspondence ceased, and Monmouth was later dropped from the council.

William was aware of the many contacts with James amongst those in high places. He thought it natural that men should insure their future against a failure of the revolution, but he had no intention of allowing that to happen. Nor did he countenance treason. When, at the very end of 1690, John Ashton and Lord Preston were intercepted carrying letters depicting a country ripe for counter-revolution and specifically suggesting that the seamen were disloyal and that Richard Carter, who commanded the *Vanguard*, and other sea officers were unsteady, Ashton was executed, while Preston saved his life by giving away other Jacobite conspirators.

Dartmouth was amongst those committed to the Tower a second time, and he died there in October 1691 at the age of 43. Dalrymple alleges that Dartmouth had offered to man ships in James's interest if the French king would sail them with skeleton crews to the English coast in winter. Not unnaturally Louis declined to hazard his ships in this fashion for so intangible a gain. Dartmouth certainly provided hard intelligence to the enemy in the form of a list of the fleet found amongst the intercepted correspondence.

The Jacobites were not the only danger to William and Mary. At the turn of the year, sensing the danger to their own cause of any rival to the throne, they betrayed a plot to place Anne on the throne and to drive out the Dutch from high places in the realm. Marlborough, suspected centre of this movement owing to his attachment to the Princess through her friendship with his wife, was deprived of all his offices in the January of 1692. Nevertheless, as 1691 ended both Louis and James were beginning to believe that a large measure of support for their cause would be forthcoming if put to the test. The Princess Anne had addressed a letter of submission and repentance to her father in December. It appeared that she might answer for the Church, Marlborough for the army, Russell for the fleet. It was this belief of the two kings, based as much on wishful thinking as on faulty intelligence, that led to the confrontation of the following year.

Chapter 5

*Kneller: Edward Russell with his finger on the globe at the coast of
Normandy, scene of his triumph* (The National Maritime Museum,
London).

Danger   *Spring 1692*

The king left for the Continent in March 1692, accompanied on this occasion by William Blathwayt, who had shown all the persistence of a vicar of Bray in clinging to the office of Secretary-at-War. Blathwayt had been in the same post when James faced William uncertainly at Salisbury, but he was now serving the new king with equal zeal, and William found of particular value the knowledge of languages possessed by his acting Secretary of State.

For this year's campaign William was determined to use his army, as Carmarthen had suggested in the previous July, for a descent on France. The allies in Champagne, Savoy, Spain and the Netherlands were all being successfully held on the frontiers. The way through Normandy was open if an army of sufficient strength could be successfully landed and maintained. Before he sailed, escorted by Shovell in the *Prince* with seven 3rd-rates, the king gave instructions that preparations should be made for the attack at the end of May or early June. Russell was directed to concert the plans with the military commanders Leinster and Galway; they met several times, and received topographical intelligence about possible targets from a French refugee. It did not take long for the project to become general knowledge: before the end of March Evelyn was recording 'much discourse of our intended descent in France this campaign'.[1]

Delaval's winter squadron reached the Downs on 18 March. Released from the task of watching the Shannon, he had been ordered to escort the Straits convoy. There were 48 ships for Oporto and 15 for Lisbon awaiting convoy early in December, and Delaval sailed with them and others in January. Orders were sent to him to avoid Cape St Vincent and to return to Dingle Bay in south-west Ireland, but they missed him, and it was just as well that they did. Naval strength in the Channel was soon to be all important. With his flag in the *York*, Delaval reached Cadiz on 26 January, and sailed homeward on 21 February with a convoy of 70 English and Dutch merchant vessels. On 11 March he was in sight of Land's End, and four days later Nottingham was writing to Blathwayt that 'Sir Ralph Delaval is arrived in safety and with a diligence and punctuality becoming so good an officer.'[2] The lesson of 1690, when Killigrew had failed to return in time for his ships to join the Grand Fleet, had been taken well to heart. The effect was somewhat spoiled when Delaval's flagship ran aground in the Thames estuary on the way up river, and was forced to jettison many of her guns to get off.

For Russell in London the chief task was to find men for the fleet. Throughout January and February he was issuing orders to the yachts to scour the coasts, from Newcastle in the north to Bideford in the west, in search of seamen. In reply to a Scottish complaint about the impressment of Scots, the king gave orders in January that the practice was to stop. But he pointed out that both kingdoms were equally threatened, and told the Scottish authorities to raise 1,000 seamen. The men would be paid a bounty of 40 shillings on entry to the Royal Navy, and would thereafter earn the same wages as English seamen. Rather belatedly on 17 March the administration ordered a general imprest, and at the end of April the queen instructed Russell 'to send orders to all tenders belonging to the fleet to press seamen in the way'.[3] He had been doing it since early January.

In March the Admiralty ordered the two Marine regiments to march to Chatham, and Russell told Ashby, who as admiral of the blue was the senior officer in the Thames and Medway, to allocate one to the red squadron and one to his own. At the end of the month Russell reported the fleet still short of 5,000 men; the two regiments would cut this figure by 1,200.

The regiment allotted to the red squadron was commanded by Peregrine Osborne, Carmarthen's third and eldest surviving son, who had taken the title of Earl of Danby on his father's elevation. He also held a commission to command the 90-gun *Windsor Castle* in Rooke's division of the blue squadron, and had commanded the *Resolution* of 70 guns during the previous summer. He was a colourful character, who inspired confidence among his men, as evidenced by the fact that 200 seamen had volunteered to transfer with him from one ship to another. He was interested in attaining speed under sail, and had earlier fitted out a yacht which he had intended using as a privateer, a project prevented by his father. It was he who had provided a similar fast craft, on loan to him from Grafton at the end of 1690, to effect the arrest off Tilbury of Ashton and Preston as they cowered with their treasonable correspondence beneath the hatch of a smack.

With the onset of spring the initiative passed to the French. Tourville had found a different atmosphere when he reached Court after the frustrating summer cruise of 1691. The Marquis de Louvois, who as Minister of War had opposed all plans for invasion of England, was dead. Louis, encouraged by James and by optimistic plans prepared by his Intendant-General of Marine, decided to take advantage of the customary late concentration of the allied fleets to make a landing in England before the Dutch squadron had joined. James originally favoured a short sea crossing with embarkation symbolically at Ambleteuse, where he had landed in 1688, but the bulk of the forces were already gathered in the Cotentin peninsula of Normandy, and the decision was made to embark the infantry at la Hougue and the cavalry at le Havre.

The Irish troops, paid and re-equipped at the expense of the French treasury after arriving in rags, had formed nine regiments of infantry, each of two battalions, besides two regiments of foot-dragoons, two of cavalry and two companies of body-guards for James under Berwick and Sarsfield, now Earl of Lucan. Although, in his exasperation after the Boyne, James had said publicly that he would never again entrust his fate to an Irish army, his incurable optimism made him glad enough to place himself at the head of this force, which was strengthened by French troops in about equal numbers, and commanded by the French marshal de Bellefonds.

Shipping began to assemble to transport the army, and d'Estrées set sail from Toulon with a squadron of warships to act as close escort, while Tourville was to prevent any interference by the English fleet, the Dutch being assumed to be still at their home ports. But d'Estrées made a slow passage, and was at first unable to pass the straits of Gibraltar, suffering much damage and losing two ships in a storm off Ceuta. One was a 70-gun ship, the other a 64. About 250 men were drowned, and 500 became prisoners of the Spanish.

Tourville had been subjected to the same sort of sniping as had Russell, and had been constrained to write an account of his services to France, detailing each action, each prize, each shipwreck – rather in the manner of St Paul in his second epistle to the Corinthians, but with greater circumstantial detail. He boasted, and it was a boast that was to come horribly home, that it was he who had first burnt enemy vessels under their fortresses. When his coach brought him to Brest in April he was well aware of the expectations centred on him at Court. Louis had himself presided at the council which formed and approved the final plan. The admiral had replied with a negative monosyllable when the king asked whether one could anchor behind the Goodwins whence one could see the entrance to the Thames, but had been more emphatic in his opposition when asked about attacking the fleet anchorage at St Helen's. The council decided on a descent at Torbay. Tourville was to embark 200 troops in each of his warships at la Hougue, and was to escort the rest of the army in transports. He was then to return to Brest, to be reinforced by the divisions from Rochefort and Toulon, and to prevent any interference by the English fleet.

Time was of the essence if this were to be accomplished before the Dutch joined. 'You would anger the King,' the minister wrote to him, 'if, on pretext of wanting explanations on the orders received, you were to postpone your departure by a single tide.' Then, as to his adversary Torrington at Beachy Head, came the final order, impossible to disobey. His Majesty wished him to leave Brest on 25 April, 'even though he receives word that the enemy are outside with a superior number of ships. In case he meets them on passage to la Hougue,' the minister continued, 'His Majesty wishes him to engage, whatever their strength.' Beneath Pontchartrain's signature the king added this fatal passage: 'I add this word in my own hand to this instruction in order to tell you that what it contains is my will and I wish it to be exactly followed.' Tourville was told not to discuss the king's orders, but to execute them; if he would not do so, the king would replace him with someone more obedient and less circumspect. He summoned his flag officers and told them that, already accused of circumspection, they must not lay themselves open to a charge of cowardice.[4]

James had left St Germains for la Hougue on 21 April to join Marshal Bellefonds' army. He and the marshal formed an invasion committee with Bonrepaus, the senior Intendant of Marine, who was considered an expert on English capabilities because of a visit to London as ambassador in 1686 and an inspection of Portsmouth with James two years later. Louis, on his way from Versailles to Flanders, boasted at Chantilly: 'There will be a great sea battle'.

In England the French preparations were at first thought to be directed against the Channel Islands. The newly promoted rear admiral of the blue, Richard Carter, who was about to sail with a small squadron for the protection of the inward trade from Spain and Portugal, was given new orders on 13 April. Before he could sail, the true destination of the enemy invasion force became known to the English Government, after a French sloop carrying letters had run on the Goodwins, and had been taken by a boat from the *Swiftsure*. The battalion originally intended for passage in Carter's ships to reinforce the garrison of Guernsey was therefore disembarked on orders from London. With eight ships, a fireship and two small craft, Carter anchored off Guernsey on the 27th, and found the population apprehensive. Monmouth, who had been sent with him as Governor of Guernsey to put the place in a posture of defence, instructed him to land bread and meat for the small garrison. The celebration of the queen's birthday on the 30th was marred by a fatal accident on board the 50-gun *Deptford*. A surgeon's mate, answering a call of nature in the heads and unaware that a salute would be fired, was killed when a chase gun was discharged.

Local intelligence that St Malo was empty was so firm that Carter decided not to investigate the place. He confirmed the Government's intelligence on 5 May when, after his ships had been carried through the Alderney race on the flood tide, the *Centurion* captured a French privateer of eight guns after a short chase. Although the French successfully threw overboard the packet they were carrying from le Havre to Brest, a prisoner disclosed the preparations being made for embarking a Franco-Irish army at la Hougue and le Havre, and that James himself was in Normandy. Carter's reconnaissance of la Hougue roads on 8 May was hindered by an easterly wind and hazy weather; he therefore crossed the Channel, and found another squadron under Delaval at St Helen's next day.

Delaval, vice admiral of the red, had been ordered by Russell on 26 April to sail from the Nore with all the 3rd-rates and smaller vessels, and to pass within sight of Calais, Dieppe, St Valéry and le Havre. Later orders were sent to him from London to cruise between the Isle of Wight and Cap de la Hague 'as the properest station at which Mr. Russell might come to him'.[5]

Delaval sailed from the Nore with his flag in the *Berwick* on the 26th, writing to Nottingham as he did so that he was in an ill condition for scouts, the perennial complaint of British admirals down the centuries. Though he had 16 3rd-rates, he had but a single ship of the 4th rate. The squadron spent the whole of the next day stormbound at anchor in the Gunfleet with yards struck, while Nottingham was telling the Admiralty to reinforce it with ships of the 3rd rate and anything smaller.

It was 3 May before it stood south-south-east from Rye Bay, 26 ships by then, with a brigantine and three fireships, to sight the French shore, chasing some fishing boats before it. The *Oxford* and *Portsmouth* galley went close inshore off Fécamp, and the *Oxford*'s barge ventured even closer, but there was nothing to be done. The *Crown* and the brigantine looked into the mouth of the Seine on 5 May, and later made a reconnaissance of le Havre, having great difficulty in withdrawing from a lee shore in a strong tidal stream. Commanding officers were subsequently told that there were few ships there, and nothing worthy of what was likely to prove a hazardous operation.

There was a flurry on 6 May when the *Dragon*, which had been scouting ahead, came back with her topgallant sails flying. The ships cleared for action, but no enemy fleet was sighted. It seems that the *Dragon* had mistaken a Swedish and Danish convoy for the French fleet. The convoy had a fair wind up Channel, and passed ahead without further contact as Delaval steered north. The assembled captains concluded that it would be prudent to stay on the English side of the Channel. On 8 May the squadron anchored off St Helen's, and watched Carter's ships come in next day.

William's doubts about the possibility of a French invasion had been overcome before the end of April by the strength and detail of reports reaching him from all sides. He realized that an assault could only be prevented by getting the Dutch fleet to sea, and lamented the contrary winds which kept it in its home ports. He went to the Hague himself early in May, ready to return to England, and sent Portland to reassure his wife that he would come over if he heard of a French landing. Later in the month, when he rejoined the allied army near Brussels, he kept a yacht and escorts standing by on the coast. In England all efforts were concentrated on repelling invasion, and all preparations for the English descent on the French coast were at a standstill. One result, which was to have serious repercussions, was that seamen were pressed from military transports to man the fleet, so that troops required for the operation could not move from Ireland.

Russell himself remained as late as possible in London, visiting the fleet from time to time, and issuing orders through his secretary Josiah Burchett at Covent Garden. On 9 April he gave his standing instructions to Delaval and Shovell, his vice and rear admirals in the red squadrons, and told Ashby to pass them on to his inferior flag officers, Rooke and Carter, in the blue. Flag officers were to visit each ship in their divisions once every ten days, they were to see them well manned, rigged, stored and provisioned, and that the crews were not oppressed by poor food. On 12 April he gave orders to the *Dolphin* at Plymouth to sail at once for the French coast to gain intelligence of the French fleet. She obtained it from three Danish vessels, and reported the enemy fleet 'near 40 sail in all' in Brest harbour and roadstead. The French, it was said, had been forced to embark boys of 12 years of age. 'If true,' commented Russell, 'the French are not much to be feared.'[6]

The Dutch, hastened by William, were expected by 22 April, and a council of war decided on the 14th to await them at the flats of the foreland, but it was not till the 27th that Russell gave the order for Ashby to sail there from the Nore with any ships of the first three rates that were ready. He himself remained a few more days in London, took leave of the queen on the 29th, and started down river by yacht on 3 May. At noon, when he was already under sail, he received word that the queen wished to see him that afternoon. He already had his orders – to join Delaval and to prevent any descent by destroying the enemy transports. If the French fleet was in superior strength he was to hinder an enemy descent until reinforced sufficiently to give battle. Russell saw no reason to turn back, and went on board the *Britannia* at the Nore early next morning.

The fleet immediately unmoored and started moving towards the north foreland, arriving there on the afternoon of the 6th, chased by a letter from Nottingham advising the commander-in-chief that the French fleet was at sea, and urging him to sail. Then on 7 May Russell took advantage of fair weather and a favourable wind to lead his fleet through the Gull stream inside the Goodwin sands to the Downs, a feat for which he has been praised, and to which his subsequent success has been attributed. Benbow was with him as master of the fleet, and possibly contributed his advice in favour of this courageous decision, though his political opponents were later to allege that it was made 'against the opinion of all the pilots with so great hazard of the fleet that he says . . . he was very lucky'.[7] He may indeed have thought himself lucky, but no operations of war, or naval operations at any time, are conducted without some hazard. The mark of the good commander is to be seen in his successful calculation of risks.

The Dutch admiral and vice admiral were waiting in the Downs with most of the squadron, but Russell's ships swept through the anchorage on the fresh breeze, and the commander-in-chief could not even send a letter ashore at Deal. The Dutch followed him, and anchored off Rye three hours after the English. The Dutch contingent of Delaval's winter squadron, after refitting at Portsmouth, had been ordered to the eastward and were awaiting the fleet off Dungeness. In London Evelyn noted with relief on the 8th that the eastern winds, so constantly blowing, had given our fleet time to unite.

Orders were left with the mayor of Rye for any English or Dutch stragglers to join the fleet at its general rendezvous off St Helen's. Russell's chief concern, now that he had the great ships concentrated with Almonde's Dutch squadron, was to make sure that Delaval joined him with the bulk of the 3rd-rates. Delaval's original orders, after his cruise down the French coast, were to cross to the Isle of Wight, send in to St Helen's for orders, and, if none, to fall back to the foreland. He might be complying with them or with his later orders to cruise across the Channel. Russell spread four small vessels to look out, so that there should be little chance of missing him. A gale on the 10th kept all ships at anchor off the south coast with their topmasts and yards down. They got them up next day, and on the evening of the 12th ran before a strong north-easterly wind, with single foresails set, to anchor at St Helen's, where Delaval's and Carter's squadrons awaited them. On the same day Russell sent off seven small vessels to look for the enemy, three to cruise between Portland and the Caskets, a group of rocks west of Alderney, two between the Isle of Wight and Cap de la Hague at the north-western tip of the Cotentin peninsula, and two off the cape itself. Two Dutch frigates were added a couple of days later.

Tourville had been at sea for ten days. His fleet began to leave harbour at Brest on 29 April, but it was held by the weather at anchor in Berteaume roads till 2 May. Even then the wind remained obstinately easterly. There was some truth in the report that had reached Russell of manning difficulties in the French fleet. Tourville's orders did not permit him to tarry longer: he left Château-Renault behind to complete the crews of 20 ships still wanting 2,000 men. He had only 37 warships and seven fireships, but off Plymouth on 15 May he was joined by Villette from Rochefort to bring his fleet up to 44 ships of the line with 11 fireships. His presence off the coast of Devon had been reported earlier than this. Russell knew on the 12th that the enemy fleet was off the Start on the 8th. The post boy with this news arrived at Southampton from Salisbury without his packet, and had to ride back seven miles to find it by the roadside. Mees of the *Ruby* had picked up further intelligence – that Tourville with 56 ships was expected at la Hougue to escort the troops to England.

In spite of all the efforts made, some of Russell's ships were still very poorly manned. Mason of the *Vanguard* reported to Ashby on 16 May that he had 612 men on board, of whom only 220 were able seamen; the rest were ordinary seamen, and 150 of those had never been to sea before. A week earlier he had complained how pitifully his ship was manned even after picking up 80 pressed men from a tender off Dover. By sending a lieutenant to Weybridge he had obtained 27 men pressed by the Deputy Lieutenant for Surrey. Other promises of 200 men from a frigate at Deptford and 150 from the Hudson's Bay Company resulted in additions far short of the numbers mentioned. There was little enough time to knock such a company into shape, and make it fit to sail the ship and fight her guns. But a return showed that half a dozen ships were over-manned, and set Russell grumbling about having to re-distribute the men, penalizing the diligent and popular captains. 'The fighting part,' he complained, 'is by much the least trouble that an Admiral of the English Fleet meets with.'[8]

Russell had issued his line of battle with his sailing orders on 4 May, but on Sunday evening, 15 May, he called all captains on board the *Britannia* to discuss it. The whole fleet made a most formidable force. Divided as usual into red, white and blue squadrons, it was to be led by the Dutch white when on the starboard tack, and by the English blue when on the port tack.

The Dutch, with further ships joining on 13 and 14 May, had managed to muster 26 ships of rates fit to lie in the line (see Appendix 1), in spite of losing one 70-gun ship which ran ashore leaving the Texel. Almonde, with the rank of Luitenant-Admiraal, flew his flag in the 92-gun *Prins*, one of the eight great ships corresponding to the first two English rates; he had three vice admirals; and there were three rear admirals with the curious rank of 'schout-by-nacht'. This title, dating from 1614, indicated its holder's duty of providing a night look-out at the rear of the squadron. The Dutch were rather better off for small craft than the English, with 13 frigates and six despatch vessels, as well as seven fireships.

The red and blue squadrons each had eight ships of the first two rates, and were thus equal to the white in great ships, though slightly superior in total numbers (see Appendix 2).

Sir Ralph Delaval was vice admiral of the red squadron, his flag transferred from his temporary flagship the 3rd-rate *Berwick* to the *Royal*

Sovereign of 100 guns; the rear admiral was Sir Cloudisley Shovell with his flag in the 100-gun *Royal William*, renamed in April after many years of royal service as the *Prince*. Matthew Aylmer and George Churchill commanded the only other 1st-rates in the squadron, the *London* and *St Andrew*. Churchill had been rehabilitated after getting into serious trouble through demanding payment in return for safe convoy, a despicable action, even when measured by the standards of public morality in seventeenth-century England.

Though he did not know it, Churchill owed the retention of his command at this moment to his commander-in-chief's firm handling of confidential exchanges with Nottingham. When Churchill's brother Marlborough was arrested on 5 May, Russell was directed to give him the unwelcome news, but to assure him that the queen relied on his fidelity. Two days later she had second thoughts: she intimated that she thought that Churchill should not be trusted in command of a 1st-rate, and suggested that he might be sent to London on some pretext of business. The letter conveying this message crossed with one from Russell reporting that he had told Churchill of the queen's favourable opinion. The captain had asked that Her Majesty be assured that he would never give cause to bring himself under suspicion. Russell ignored the second letter; he was ready to pawn the little credit he possessed for George Churchill's faithful service; he would not displace him without a further order. With that the queen was content.

The flag officers of the blue squadron were Admiral Sir John Ashby, Vice Admiral George Rooke and Rear Admiral Richard Carter. Ashby carried his flag in the *Victory*; Rooke was in the *Neptune*, Carter in the *Duke*. John Tyrrel commanded the 90-gun *Ossory* in Carter's division; his reputation had been untarnished by the loss of the 70-gun *Anne* at Beachy Head. After losing all his masts in action he had been forced ashore with hull damage in Rye Bay. The French had sent two fireships to finish off his ship, but he had burnt her himself. There were four other 90-gun ships in the squadron.

Each squadron contained a good number of 3rd-rates of 70 or 60 guns, the work-horses of the fleet, and a few 4th-rates of 50 guns. Each division had three or four fireships in attendance, besides yachts and ketches. The fleet was augmented by frigates and galleys of the 5th and 6th rates, too small to lie in the line, but useful as scouts and despatch vessels.

It is ironic that the English fleet preparing to secure William against displacement by 'the rightful king' should have contained among its ships so many reminders of James and his brother: the *Monk*, named after the architect of the Restoration, the *Albemarle*, after his later title; the *Montagu* and *Sandwich*, after another Stuart admiral, and the *Rupert*, after a third; the *Restoration*; and the *Monmouth*, *Grafton* and *Berwick*, named after royal bastards. Monmouth, of course, had been executed for attempting to wrest the crown from his uncle James, and the title had been given by William to Mordaunt; Grafton had been killed in action at Cork in the previous autumn; and Berwick, sole survivor of the trio, waited with the Franco-Irish army encamped near la Hougue. The *Northumberland, Lennox* and *St Albans* commemorated three more of Charles II's illegitimate sons.

As his first captain on board the *Britannia*, Russell had David Mitchell, who had first gone to sea as an apprentice in a merchant vessel, and who had been pressed into the Royal Navy from a ship in the Baltic trade during the second Dutch war. He had obtained his first command in 1683, and had commanded a 70-gun ship at Beachy Head. Now he was the senior representative in the fleet of the type known as 'tarpaulins', to distinguish them from the sea officers of gentle birth. He was included in all meetings of flag officers, and signed any paper in which they gave their collective opinion. The commander-in-chief also relied on the skill and unbroken experience as seaman and pilot of John Benbow, a man of his own age, who had gone to sea as a master's mate in 1678, and had been made a master in the following year. He had served on the Mediterranean station under Herbert, Rooke and Shovell. After eight years in merchant vessels he had been given two commands of royal ships after the revolution, and had served Torrington as master of the fleet, as already related. Russell had the services of Josiah Burchett to assist him with the considerable amount of paper work. This man had been dismissed by Pepys after seven years as a clerk in the Admiralty. The retirement of his former master had enabled him to find new employment as Russell's clerk.

Although he had taken routine precautions against surprise, in what he always rightly regarded as a necessary part of discipline for a sea commander, Russell did not really expect a fleet action now that the English and Dutch fleets were joined. Off Rye on the 9th he urged Nottingham not to neglect the preparations for an allied descent, 'for should the French think it to their interest to avoid a battle I know of no other way to compel them to it'.[9]

It was a point to which he reverted four days later at St Helen's, when he recommended a descent on St Malo in order to force the French to a battle. If victorious, the fleet could re-embark the army and go for Brest. It was a natural appreciation for the admiral to make after his experiences of the previous summer. But he had reckoned without the dictatorial intervention of the French King.

In view of their disagreements of the previous autumn and the serious quarrel that was to come, it is interesting to read the expressions of warm regard in the correspondence passing between Nottingham and Russell at this time. Thus Russell on 1 May: 'I return you ten thousand thanks for your kind advice yesterday and the assurance of your friendship, which I assure you I most extremely value and covet, and I will endeavour not to forfeit the favourable opinion you have of me.' And Nottingham on the 11th: 'I am so truly your friend that I shall take it very ill if you think any man more so.'[10] These words and phrases, making allowance for seventeenth-century love of flattery, do not seem to be those of two political opponents putting on an appearance of unity in face of the common enemy. On the contrary, they appear to be genuine expressions of good will between men sharing a healthy respect for each other's qualities.

There were further political developments before the Grand Fleet could leave its anchorage off the Isle of Wight. James had taken two initiatives, equally mistaken and destined to do his cause more harm than good.

At the end of March he had despatched invitations to selected persons to attend the next confinement of his queen, expected about mid-May, in an effort to avoid the monstrous charges of substitution that had been made and had received wide credence after the birth of the Prince of Wales. Even his daughters Mary and Anne were bidden, with other noble ladies and members of the Privy Council. Safe conduct was guaranteed by the French King. The invitations were universally ignored. Anne was in any event going through her seventh pregnancy; it ended sadly with the death of a boy immediately after birth. She nevertheless wrote again to her father promising to fly to his side on his arrival in England. The queen too was unwell for a week with a feverish cold after Easter, missing church attendance on Sunday for the first time in 12 years, but she recovered in time to play a decisive role in protecting the kingdom from invasion. Not so dramatic as Queen Elizabeth I's appearance at Tilbury a century earlier, it was none the less effective.

James's second action had been to issue a proclamation of his intentions when restored – he would establish religious toleration, there would be a political amnesty except for those on a published list of traitors. Mary, who was now proving herself a mistress of political affairs, arranged for James's proclamation to be given the widest publicity, accompanied by a Government commentary on each of its provisions.

Then she dealt in her own way with the allegations of disaffection in the English fleet. Nottingham sent to St Helen's a personal message from her to be read to the flag officers and captains. She did not believe the rumours, she declared, and knew that the officers would fight as became Englishmen for their country. The senior officers, assembled on board the *Britannia* on 15 May, unanimously signed a declaration of loyalty to the Crown, the Protestant religion and the freedom of England. 'And that God Almighty may preserve Your Majesty's most sacred person,' they concluded, 'direct your counsels, and prosper your arms by sea and by land against Your Majesty's enemies, let all your people say Amen with Your Majesty's most dutiful and loyal subjects.' The queen's gracious reply, 'that she always had this opinion of the commanders, but was glad this was come to satisfy others', was published in the *London Gazette* next day. Mary was becoming equally a mistress of public relations, though privately she admitted that she had not 'much opinion of what would be done at sea by Mr. Russell'; she hoped he would do better than last year.[11]

Whereas in the previous year the fleet would have met the French on almost equal terms, it now enjoyed a superiority of almost two to one over Tourville. The squadron of d'Estrées from the Mediterranean had still not arrived at Brest. Tourville, hindered by the persistent easterly winds, was still attempting to beat up Channel. Pontchartrain, the Minister of Marine, was becoming anxious. He sent off a despatch to d'Estrées urging him not to lose a moment, and explaining that Tourville was in the Channel much inferior in strength. On 9 May he countermanded the king's orders to fight *fort ou faible*, but it was too late; the fresh orders did not reach Tourville in time to stop him.

The French line of battle was only 44 ships strong, but 11 of them mounted more than 80 guns (see Appendix 3). Tourville's flagship was still the *Soleil Royal* of 104 guns, as in the previous year, and he commanded the white squadron himself. The Marquis d'Amfreville, one of six marquises among the flag and commanding officers, commanded the white and blue squadron from the 94-gun *Merveilleux*, and the blue squadron was under Gabaret in the *Orgueilleux*, which carried the same number of guns. The subordinate flag officers were Villette in the *Ambitieux* and Langeron in the *Souverain* in Tourville's squadron; Nesmond in the *Monarque* and Relingue in the *Foudroyant* under d'Amfreville; and Coëtlogon in the *Magnifique* and Pannetier in the *Grand* under Gabaret. Fifteen of the captains were knights, and the rank of *commandeur*, borne by the commanding officer of the *Brillant*, was a reminder of the close ties between the French Navy and the Order of St John. On 17 May this fleet, which with its fireships and auxiliaries numbered between 70 and 80 sail, appeared again off the English coast at Portland.

The threat of invasion had been treated seriously in England. Evelyn wrote before the end of April of 'great talk of the French invasion and of an universal rising', and on 5 May: 'the reports of an invasion being now so hot, alarmed the city, court and people exceedingly'. There was universal consternation, he added.[12] There was indeed the usual round-up of suspected Jacobites, all papists were ordered to move at least ten miles from London, soldiers were encamped between Petersfield and Portsmouth, the trained bands and militia were called out, and instructions given that all cattle were to be driven 15 miles from any part of the coast where the French fleet appeared.

There was nothing to detain Russell after the declaration of loyalty had been despatched; the sooner the allied fleet was at sea the better. He had no new instructions from Whitehall; the threat was obvious and his duty clear. The fleet unmoored and weighed anchor on 16 May, but only moved a few miles in light airs before anchoring again. The same thing was repeated on the 17th, when three light craft brought in a French fishing boat taken in the Channel. At last on the 18th Russell received definite intelligence of the enemy fleet from the captain of a Guernsey privateer which had passed through it in fog. At five in the morning the allied fleet weighed and set sail on the starboard tack with a fresh south-westerly wind. An hour later Russell made the signal for the line of battle, and by noon the fleet was 15 miles from the Isle of Wight, with the frigate *Chester* and the *Charles* galley spread to the westward as look-outs. Even at this late stage the *Royal Catherine*'s ketch joined her parent ship from the westward with about 140 men.

News that the French were off Portland had reached Nottingham at Whitehall at three in the morning. The messenger with an express from the clerk of the parish of Weymouth had ridden 106 miles in 16 hours. Another express, despatched at the same time by the mayor to Portsmouth, brought the news to the fleet as it was leaving its anchorage. To those anxiously awaiting the outcome in the capital it appeared that it had sailed in time to forestall an invasion, especially when a frigate brought in three prizes, and intelligence that the French transports were not yet ready. The fleet stood to the southward all night, the Dutch leading and the blue squadron in the rear, but it was not possible to maintain the line in conditions of darkness, even in fair weather.

At four next morning there was a light breeze from the south-west. The French fleet was steering north-east in six columns under easy sail about 21 miles north of Cap Barfleur at the eastern tip of the Cotentin peninsula. As dawn broke the allied fleet was sighted, about nine miles to leeward, by the 64-gun *Henri* and, as the mist cleared, it became visible in all its might to the whole French fleet. Tourville came round to the starboard tack like the allies and lay to in order to call a council of war of his flag officers. Assessed at this time by the young Berwick as the cleverest seaman in France and perhaps in the whole world, Tourville must have realized that more than his reputation was at stake. He could not carry out his orders to embark and escort the troops to England without first defeating the allied fleet, but since the invasion plan was based on achieving the landing before the English and Dutch fleets united, it was already a dead letter. Nevertheless he still felt piqued at the aspersions that had been made after the preceding campaign, and was conscious of the prodding he had received from the king and his Minister. There were, too, the reports of disaffection in the English fleet; perhaps some ships would refuse to fight, and would rally to the Stuart standard at la Hougue.

Though some later authorities have questioned whether the council of war ever took place, Tourville himself records it, and the French historian Sué has given a graphic description of this meeting in the great cabin of the *Soleil Royal*, superbly furnished with console tables and *fauteuils* of carved gilded wood, and hangings of red, silver and gold brocades. Tourville walked up and down, his hands behind his back, while his juniors sat round the council table. The French had the weather gauge, and could choose whether to fight the allies or to refuse action. The odds were plainly about two to one. Gabaret spoke for all the rest when he advised against fighting. Then Tourville showed them the king's order with its telling postscript in his own hand. There could be no gainsaying an instruction so absolute: 'I wish it to be exactly followed.' Like Torrington's admirals at Beachy Head, the French flag officers accepted the order as mandatory, and left the cabin, each shaking Tourville's hand as he departed.

The French line, though still in some confusion, was almost formed; Tourville was able to signal 'Bear down on the enemy' as soon as the flag officers had regained their ships. On board the *Prince*, Bagneux addressed his men from the poop: '*Mes enfants*, we are going at the peril of our lives to serve our religion, our country and our king.' The chaplain advised them to get down on their knees and recite the *Miserere* and *Confiteor*. They were all given a plenary indulgence and a swig of brandy; then they went to their action stations.

Between three and four in the morning, when something over 20 miles north-east of Cap Barfleur, Russell heard guns to the westward, and soon afterwards made out his two look-out vessels steering north with their topgallant sails flying to indicate that they had the enemy in sight. Thinking that the French were steering north, as indeed at first they were, he ordered his blue squadron in the rear to tack. Dawn visibility was as usual less good to the westward than to the eastward; by the time Russell sighted the enemy fleet it was steering south on the starboard tack and beginning to form into line of battle.

After making out the white colours of the French, he ordered his ships to clear for action. On board the *Vanguard*, as no doubt in other ships, they stove down the cabins and hove them overboard, not only to clear the decks for serving the guns, but also to lessen the dangers from wood splinters, one of the most common causes of wounds. The fleet flagship stood away from the enemy while other ships placed themselves in order of battle. The captain of the *Chester* reported personally on board the *Britannia* before taking up his station in the line, and Russell received another report from the commander of his second scouting vessel, the *Charles* galley.

When Russell judged, as he wrote afterwards, that 'each ship in the fleet might fetch my wake or grain', that is, that each ship could take her appointed station either astern or ahead of the flagship, he ordered the *Britannia* to lie to;[13] she remained motionless on the calm sea, her foresail backed against the mast, while the rest of the ships endeavoured to reach their allotted positions. By eight there was a tolerably good line running from the Dutch van to the south-south-westward to the rear of the red squadron, though even at that stage the log of the *Cambridge*, last but one of Shovell's division, records 'we being out of order and most not being able to get into their line'. For the ships of the blue squadron were still to leeward, and had their boats out in an attempt to prolong the line north-north-east instead of tailing away to the eastward.

Tourville, with fore and main topsails and mizzen set, had begun to bear down on the centre of the allied line, keeping his own flagship headed for Russell's, while Villette in the *Ambitieux* made for the *Royal Sovereign*. The leading division of the French van under Nesmond stretched ahead with all sails set, their boats towing to keep steerage way, in order to prevent the Dutch from doubling on the French line or breaking through it, containing their superior numbers at long range. Russell had indeed ordered Almonde to tack to windward of the French, but the *Bourbon*, leading the French van, drew level with the leading Dutch ship and effectively foiled the manoeuvre. While Tourville attempted to obtain a local superiority, or at least to fight on even terms, in the centre, his rear squadron under Gabaret found its leading division opposite Shovell's division at the rear of the English red squadron, while the remainder were unopposed because the English blue squadron was not in station. Gabaret's rearmost division, under Pannetier, was in any event holding its wind so as to prevent any attempt to envelop the line at that end.

Earlier in the morning Ashby had complied with Russell's order to the blue squadron to tack, but he soon saw that in the light wind he would be unable to profit from the manoeuvre, and might indeed be prevented from playing any part in the action. He therefore came back to the starboard tack. It was this diversion that had left most of his squadron so far to leeward of the remainder of the fleet. His ships did their best to comply with the commander-in-chief's order to close up.

As Russell saw the boldness of Tourville's advance and his concentration on the *Britannia*, he feared momentarily, as he afterwards admitted, that it was true that there would be defections in the English fleet; that, as he put it, 'some of the officers was to kick'.[14] The Dutch too watched in amazement as the French appeared willing to attack a fleet of over 80 warships with 44. As Van der Putte subsequently reported to the

Admiralty of Zeeland, Tourville's conduct could only be explained by his having received an assurance that the Dutch would not have joined, and that 15 of the English ships would change sides.

By about 11 a.m. the centres of the two fleets were at musket shot distance, the *Soleil Royal* on the *Britannia*'s starboard quarter. Shovell said afterwards that he had never in his life seen enemy fleets come so near to each other before they began to fight. He sent a lieutenant to the ships in his division ordering them to fill their topsails as soon as he engaged. There was a pause of almost a quarter of an hour, as if neither side wished to be the first to open fire. Russell indeed had deliberately refrained from hoisting the red flag at the fore so as to allow Tourville, who had the weather gauge, to come as close as he desired. Then a Dutch ship fired at the *Saint-Louis* in the French van, killing a gunner, and immediately the two lines erupted into flames and smoke.

Chapter 6

Backhuisen: Barfleur. Imagination has allowed Dutch, French and English flagships to be depicted in action together (The National Maritime Museum, London).

Action 19-21 May 1692

'In a trice we were so buried in fire and smoke, and had such hot service ourselves, that we could not see or mind what others did.'[1] Thus wrote the Revd Richard Allyn, chaplain of the 50-gun *Centurion*, two ships astern of Delaval's flagship. In fact the chaplain was not present at the action, having been landed sick at Portsmouth on 12 May, and he completed his account from the captain's and lieutenant's journals. But the passage reads truly enough, and is no doubt a direct quotation from somebody who went through the nightmare of the next couple of hours.

During all that time the two lines of ships kept pounding away at each other. It was difficult to miss: if firing on the down roll, in order to hit the hull, a late ignition might put the shot in the sea; if firing on the up roll, with the object of damaging masts and rigging, the ball might pass harmlessly overhead. Otherwise, at such a range, every shot told. The smoke from so much gunpowder dispersed slowly, for what little wind there had been earlier was dying.

The *Britannia*'s rate of fire was slightly better than that of the *Soleil Royal*, and she suffered proportionately less. Two ships ahead of her lay the 50-gun *Chester*, which had signalled the enemy in sight early that morning. Outgunned by the *Glorieux*, commanded by Tourville's nephew and conspicuous because of the cross of Malta on her topsail, she was forced out of the line to repair her damage, and the next ahead, Leake's *Eagle*, fell back to fill the gap. The four or five rear ships of the Dutch squadron were also closely engaged, as were the leading ships of Carter's division of the blue squadron.

Then there occurred one of those rare chances that happen in war, to be taken or missed, like a catch at cricket, according to the quality of the commander. Shovell seized it. About an hour after noon the wind came round, from the light airs between west and west-south-west that had persisted since dawn, to a slight breeze from north-west. In other words, it veered about 50 degrees and freshened a little. Shovell ordered his flagship to luff up to the new breeze, and as she did so she broke through the French line ten ships from the tail, separating Gabaret and Pannetier from Coëtlogon's division of the French blue squadron. Neville in the *Kent*, next ahead of Shovell, saw what his flag officer was doing, and followed his motions, using his boats to tow his ship into station astern

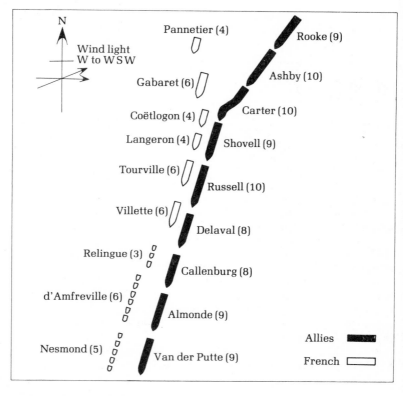

Map 2. Barfleur: 19 May 11.00 hrs

instead of ahead of the rear admiral on the new course. The *St Albans*, ahead of the *Kent*, and the ships astern of the flagship did the same, making seven ships in all, but the *Hampton Court* and *Swiftsure* remained with Russell's division. On board the *Oxford* it was not realized what had happened until the smoke cleared to reveal the main French fleet to leeward and five enemy ships to windward making what sail they could to rejoin it.

The shift of wind also gave an opportunity to the leading ships of the English blue squadron. The *Suffolk* set all the sail she could, and got to windward of two ships of the enemy rear. It was warm work for the next two hours, but most of the French shot passed overhead, damaging the *Suffolk*'s masts, rigging and sails.

The Dutch too took advantage of the changed wind to force the leading French ships round. Almonde had been attempting, since the start of the action, to carry out Russell's order to tack ahead of the French fleet, but the lightness of the breeze, coupled with the French tactic of 'refusing' their van by keeping it at long range, had prevented him. With the change of wind, the Dutch were able to break through the French line, cutting off the leading ship, the *Bourbon*, and then to tack to windward of the enemy. D'Amfreville's squadron was thus forced to tack to the northward, concentrating the French van and centre, and bringing some relief to Tourville.

Shovell says that 'from that moment they began to run'.[2] The *Soleil Royal* had lost her main topsail, so she loosed her mainsail, and turned away. Villette's flagship, the *Ambitieux*, had also had enough of the *Royal Sovereign*'s fire, but before she turned she was able to concentrate her fire on the little 50-gun *Centurion* and inflict severe damage. The *Centurion*'s casualties were seven killed and 18 wounded, mostly with leg wounds. Her longboat had been sunk at her stern, and a gun had split on her quarter-deck, causing some self-inflicted casualties, a constant hazard in war and battle. A similar accident killed 20 men on board the *Saint-Louis* in the opposite line. The *Eagle* was also in a bad way, and had to be ordered out of the line. All her topmasts had gone, the mizzen mast had fallen on deck, the mainmast was damaged; 70 men had been killed and twice that number wounded. Stephen Martin, Leake's first lieutenant and relative by marriage (they had married sisters), knew what it was like to be wounded. His left thigh had been broken at Bantry Bay, and he would have lost the leg had he allowed the surgeon to have his way. In this action he had two narrow escapes. The *Grafton*, at the rear of Russell's division, was considerably damaged, with some 80 casualties and several guns dismounted.

In the opposite line Forbin's *Perle* had been shot through and through; one third of his crew were casualties. The *Henri*, next ahead of Villette, was out of action, and ahead of her the *Fort* had got out sweeps in an effort to escape. These two ships had suffered severely as they tried to plug the gap which had opened between them and the rear ship of Relingue's division. They were lucky to escape. The *Henri* was saved from falling into the English line when Villette, realizing her predicament, sent a barge from another ship to tow her clear.

On board the *Brillant*, rear ship of the French van squadron, the lieutenant of the lower battery went to the poop deck, where some refreshments had been laid out. 'It's pretty hot up here', remarked the sub-lieutenant of the upper battery. 'To reproach you for your weakness,' replied the lieutenant, 'I will await you in hell.' He was killed by a cannon ball as he went down the ladder from the poop. 'Oh, my God! Save me from that rendezvous!' cried the sub-lieutenant, but at that moment he was cut in two by another ball.

The *Britannia* stuck to the French fleet flagship on the new course, still

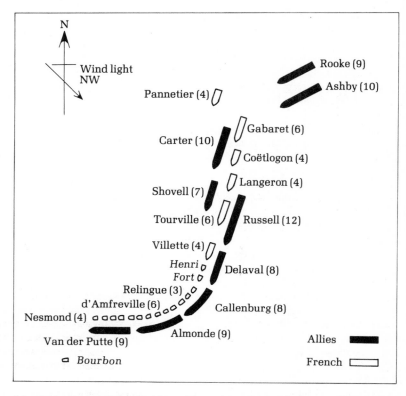

Map 3. Barfleur: 19 May 13.00 hrs. Pannetier's division is shown as four strong as in the Line of Battle: he probably had a laggard of Gabaret's division with him to make five.

supported by the *London* and *St Andrew*. On board Churchill's ship there was a woman serving as a seaman. Later in the year she turned up at Whitehall to see the queen, bearing a certificate of good conduct from the captain, and was given a suitable reward. The *Soleil Royal* was in a pitiable condition, but others came to her aid: first Coëtlogon's flagship *Magnifique*, followed by Bagneux in the *Prince*, both forced to double on the French centre by the English ships to windward. Bagneux found enemy ships on either side, while a third across the stern of his ship was raking her with shots that travelled her whole length. In half an hour the *Prince* lost 146 killed and over 60 wounded before Nesmond's flagship *Monarque*, previously near the head of the French line, came to her rescue, and other ships of the French van rallied round the fleet flagship.

This was only possible because of the Dutch action in pressing d'Amfreville's squadron. It meant that most of the French ships were now almost encircled and were concentrated in a tight bunch, all semblance of a continuous line gone, though groups of them were still in the line formation, and many were headed north on the port tack.

There was a little disorder in the English line when the *Restoration* got a puff of wind, overhauled the *Greenwich* and forced the smaller ship to leeward out of the line when she hit her a glancing blow on her starboard bow. The *Greenwich* set her foresail and luffed up to regain the line, aiming to come in between the *Britannia* and *St Andrew*, but she was ordered to drop astern. Further back the *Hampton Court*, leading ship of the two of Shovell's division still prolonging the line, had to haul out to avoid running up on the ships ahead, which were lying to with their topsails aback. She allowed her topsails to fill, overtook the *Grafton*, and regained the line astern of the *Greenwich* in the gap left by the *Restoration*. Then an enemy three-decker, probably the *Admirable*, wore out of the French line towards the *Hampton Court*, and Graydon was forced to follow her motions. He wore his ship round, using his boats to tow, and was soon in action again with his opponent on the port tack. Things were becoming rather confused after nearly five hours of fighting, and many ships had taken about as much in the way of damage and casualties as they could stand.

They were now to gain some respite, for by four o'clock it had become flat calm and very foggy. Russell found that the continuous discharge of cannon was forcing the opposing ships apart. He despatched his only written order of the day to all ships: 'Use all possible means to tow your ship into the line of battle during this calm.' He added that ships were not to go out of the line unless obliged. It is doubtful whether the order reached more than a few of the nearest ships.

The *Royal Catherine*, next ahead of the *Royal Sovereign*, took advantage of the fog and calm to tow out of the line at about four to repair her rigging. All her shrouds and stays were cut, and 22 guns were disabled. After an hour she was back in station. On board the *Centurion* word was passed to the captain that a shot through the carpenter's store had flooded the hold to a depth of seven feet. The magazine was full of water, and the powder barrels were floating in it. Ordered out of the line to careen ship and stop the leaks, her crew managed to save half of the powder barrels; the powder was so tightly packed in them that the water had caused no deterioration. In a couple of hours Wyvil's little ship was under sail to regain her station.

The centre and rear divisions of the English blue squadron were still endeavouring to join the battle, but their attention had been fixed on the five ships of the French rear under Pannetier, still separated from the rest of the enemy fleet. Shovell later criticized them for not falling on the

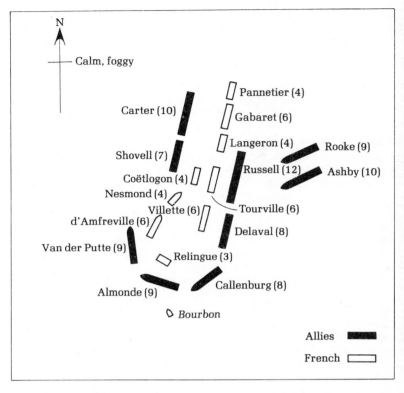

Map 4. Barfleur: 19 May 15.00 hrs

disengaged side of the main body as he and Carter had done. Tourville too was surprised to escape this added danger, and another French contemporary account refers to the waste of time by the English blue squadron. When the wind dropped and the fog came down, the divisions of Ashby and Rooke had still not fired a shot, and Pannetier had passed ahead of them to join the main body. They continued towing, though at times they could not see a ship's length.

At about five in the evening, however, the weather began to clear. The reason was a light breeze, not from a westerly direction as in the morning and early afternoon, but from the east. As the fog dispersed Russell sighted the French fleet flagship again, towed by her boats to the northward. He ordered ships of his division to tow in pursuit, and half an hour later, certain of victory as the new favourable breeze set in, told the whole allied fleet to chase. For their part the French made all the sail they could in an effort to extricate themselves, a large body of them bearing down on Carter's ships, now once more to leeward of them.

Up to that time Russell was unaware that his rear admiral had suc-ceeded in interposing his ships on the French line of retreat to the westward. When he heard guns from that direction he thought that the whole blue squadron had weathered the French rear, as he had intended at the beginning of the day. In fact Shovell's ships had fallen in with Tourville's flagship and about six other ships as soon as the fog lifted. Hearing the noise of this action to the northward, Ashby brought his two divisions round to a northerly course, putting Rooke's division ahead of his own, and again made for the sound of the guns. The whole of both fleets had crossed his front during the fog.

The French, who had not lost a ship in spite of the disparity in numbers, were not yet beaten. As they attempted to fight their way through Shovell's and Carter's ships, the weather, capricious as ever, again took a hand in events. The wind died away and the fog came down once more. When the flood set in soon after six in the evening, carrying all ships up Channel, Tourville ordered the ships of his fleet to anchor, and they did so with all sails set. It was a repetition of Torrington's successful tactic at Beachy Head two years previously, and it seems to have been Villette who reminded his admiral of it by sending an officer to propose anchoring at slack water. Tourville sent boats in each direction to carry the order along the line.

Shovell too sent a boat to direct the ships of his division to follow the French example, and most of them managed to ride just clear of the French, the *Royal William* ahead and the *Oxford* on the starboard bow of the enemy flagship, the *Kent* further to starboard. But Anthony Hastings did not have his cable clear for letting go, and suffered severely for his lack of foresight. His ship, the *Sandwich*, drifted helplessly through the French fleet, presenting her bows to raking broadsides from the *Soleil Royal*, *Magnifique* and *Saint-Philippe*. Hastings was killed, and his ship extensively damaged. Shovell, anchored up tide in the *Royal William*, with the *Kent*, *Oxford* and *St Albans*, could only fire stern chase guns at the French.

Not far away the French had anchored just before they reached Car-ter's ships, which were soon heavily engaged as the tide took them among the enemy. It was at this time that Carter lost a leg on board the *Duke*, later succumbing to his injuries. Because he had previously been the object of allegations of Jacobite leanings, historians have made much of his dying instructions to his captain to fight the ship as long as she would swim. The *Ossory*, next in line, was seldom able to fire because the *Duke* fouled her range. She only had two men killed and eight or nine wounded. All her boats were disabled, the barge being shattered to pieces and sunk while towing the ship. The barge's crew were all saved,

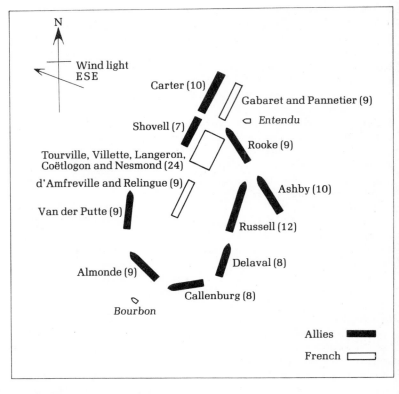

Map 5. Barfleur: 19 May 17.00 hrs

two of them severely wounded. On the French side the *Fier* suffered most heavily in this encounter.

At about seven there was sufficient wind to bring the rest of the blue squadron into action at last. Rooke in the *Neptune*, followed by the *Windsor Castle* and *Expedition*, found Shovell's ships separated from the rest of the red squadron by numbers of French ships firing their head chase guns, while Shovell's fired their stern chase guns. Rooke's three ships were soon engaged with the group of enemy ships at anchor, almost wrecking the already damaged *Soleil Royal* and *Ambitieux*. The *Northumberland*, taking the *Royal William*'s place, gave the enemy seven broadsides. The other blue division came up soon afterwards. From the *Victory*'s deck, as Ashby's flagship was towed towards the firing, Shovell's flag was suddenly seen above the fog. Within a few minutes the *Victory* was in action with the main body of the French, supported by

the *Vanguard*, *Warspite* and *Montagu*. In an engagement lasting about two
hours the *Montagu* was hit many times aloft, having her main yard split
in two, her masts and all her rigging damaged.

Shovell had meanwhile attempted to dislodge the French from their
anchors by sending down fireships. Two of them, well directed towards
the *Soleil Royal*, were towed clear by French boats in charge of lieutenants. The heat from their flames was intense; those on the deck of the
French fleet flagship could scarcely turn their faces towards the blazing
hulks as they passed. A third, towed into position by the *Cambridge*,
caused Tourville's flagship and some others to cut their cables, but all
were able to keep clear of danger, and to re-anchor. The crews of the
Ambitieux and *Magnifique* watched two fireships pass harmlessly by. One
fell aboard the *Perle*, but Forbin, who had been wounded in the knee,
managed with some difficulty to free his ship.

After the failure of the fireship attack, Shovell found that Gabaret's
and Pannetier's fresh divisions of the French rear squadron were driving
down upon him, and he gave orders to the ships with him to cut their
cables. They drifted through the gaps in the French line just as the
Sandwich had done earlier. Tourville later criticized this manoeuvre as a
bad mistake, and said that the French would not otherwise have
escaped. Shovell's ships, reinforced by a few of Rooke's, were until then
between most of the enemy and their bases at St Malo and Brest. But the
few English ships were in a very exposed position, and could not be
certain of holding out if the whole French fleet were to fall upon them
when the tide turned. They had seen nothing of the rest of the red
squadron or the Dutch for many hours. The incident is made much of in
French accounts and virtually ignored in those of the English, including
Shovell's and Rooke's own narratives. The ships suffered heavily as they
passed through the French at close range, the *Royal William* at a pike's
length from the *Magnifique* and *Saint-Philippe*, raked by double-shotted
broadsides and receiving damage to all her masts, her main and mizzen
yards, losing her spritsail yard and taking several shots on the water line.
The *Kent* and *Ruby* of Shovell's division, followed by the *Neptune*, *Windsor Castle* and *Expedition* of Rooke's, similarly ran the gauntlet. At least
they left the *Henri* full of holes, her masts and sails down, and most of her
crew killed or wounded.

It was now past ten at night, there was some moonlight, and the battle
of Barfleur was over. The blazing fireships were still adrift, but few who
saw them knew their identity. Nearly all ships reported a heavy explosion at about half past ten. With the wishful thinking of all combatants
the French attributed it to an English loss, while most of the English
accounts agree that a French ship was destroyed at this time, one even
identifying the victim as Gabaret's flagship, and others specifying a
three-decker. Whatever the cause of the explosion it was not fatal, for in

spite of all the firing, all the damage and all the casualties, not a ship in either line had sunk or struck her colours. The English had expended four fireships in the attack at nightfall, and another, the *Extravagant* with Delaval's division, had been burnt after a lucky enemy shot early in the action. The most likely explanation of the explosion is that one of Shovell's fireships blew up when already abandoned. Earlier in the day there had been an incident on board the *Expedition* of a similar nature to those suffered by individual French ships at Bantry Bay and Beachy Head. A gun in the forecastle split, scattering metal splinters, some of which set fire to cartridges and caused an explosion.

Tourville had fought successfully against heavy odds, and still had a chance to save his fleet. But he was in a serious predicament. Several of his ships could scarcely sail, the wind would probably come westerly again, and the fierce Channel tides would have to be used to full advantage if all were to escape the allied fleet. The Dutch squadron was a particular menace. Apart from the *Zeven Provincien*, formerly de Ruyter's famous flagship, which had lost 19 killed and had 14 badly wounded, and the *Capitein Generael* with nine killed and 30 wounded, including Rear Admiral van der Goes, the Dutch had not suffered severely, and were now in a good position to move in for the kill.

Russell had been prevented from exploiting his advantage in numbers by the skilful handling of the French van and rear, by his own misjudgment in not bearing away sufficiently to give two divisions of his rear squadron a chance to join the line, and by the vagaries of the weather. Shovell had failed to make a lasting success of the tactical advantage he had gained by dividing the French line. The two divisions of the blue squadron, whose late appearance turned the French retreat into a rout, might have done great things if their flag officers had had a clear picture of what was happening, or if they had ignored Pannetier in the early stages of the action and had concentrated on the enemy centre. In the foggy conditions of the afternoon it was perhaps inevitable that Ashby should have failed to notice that the trend of the fighting had changed to north just about the time that firing ceased.

The battle of Barfleur had demonstrated one thing very clearly: the allies were in overwhelming strength in the Channel; the French, even with d'Estrées' laggard squadron, which had at last reached Brest on the very day of the battle, and with Château-Renault's ships that had been left behind there, were in no condition to challenge them again; there could be no invasion of England. At the same time it had shown Russell the fighting qualities of the French, and the durability of their ships.

Tourville's fleet, initially outnumbered even in the centre, where there were six ships between Tourville and Villette, but eight between Russell and Delaval, had obtained local superiority when the rear division of Coëtlogon came to the rescue, so that the *Britannia* and her two seconds were at one time opposed to six enemy ships, and the *Restoration*, towards the rear of Russell's division, was at times engaged by two and even three ships simultaneously. Elsewhere the odds were reversed, but Russell later admitted that he would fear defeat if numbers were nearly equal; he was sure that the enemy ships were better, and he was afraid that they had better officers.[3]

The quality of his own officers was a matter to which he reverted a month after the battle, and it evidently gave him considerable anxiety. Most of them, he complained, were the scum of seafaring mankind, who could not earn their bread in any service but the king's. From what he had seen of the French, 'these are men who value their honour and I fear will beat those who have little regard for it'.[4]

Yet the allied fleet had shown encouraging initiative in conditions of visibility that made strict control by its flag officers very difficult, and at times impossible. There was none of that rigid adherence to the line that was to mar English performance in battle in the next century. Both English and Dutch had seen the possibility of surrounding the enemy and, aided by the fluky breeze, had achieved their aim, only to be robbed of a great victory by the poorness of the visibility, the weakness of the wind and the strength of the tide.

As darkness fell the commander-in-chief sent word to the ships near him to chase to the westward all night, and at dawn next morning hoisted the signal for general chase. The wind was still in the east, but the visibility remained poor. The wrecks of the fireships and much broken timber littered the surface of the calm sea.

Russell had been busy writing from an early hour. Before the weather cleared he sent the *Mary* galley to England with a letter for his wife and copies of his initial report for Nottingham and the Admiralty. As was to be expected, the detail of the losses inflicted on the enemy, recording as fact what was in reality only speculation, was inaccurate. But the report was not misleading in its general tenor. Russell also despatched a short note to Portland, the Dutch minister in the Cabinet. It was remarkable in not containing a single mention of the Dutch squadron, a subject which must be presumed to have been Portland's principal interest. 'I can give no particular account of things,' he wrote, 'but that the French were beaten.' Given a little clear weather he was confident of completely destroying their fleet.[5] The *Mary* made a good passage with the despatches, reaching Spithead the same evening.

It began to clear around eight, an hour after the *Mary* had gone, when the Dutch squadron was seen to the southward signalling that they had the enemy in sight. Soon afterwards the French could be made out, apparently about 33 sail some eight miles directly to leeward of Russell's ships, which were making all possible sail to catch up. He had with him most of the red squadron and Rooke's division of the blue. Shovell's

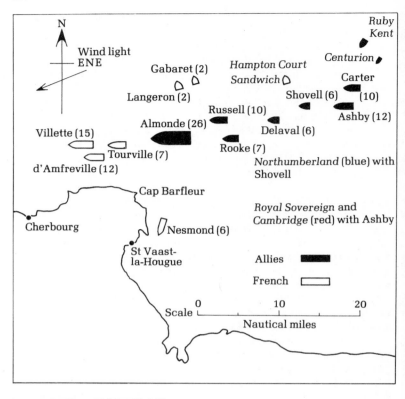

Map 6. Barfleur: 20 May 08.00 hrs.
Approximate positions to show dispersal of fleets.

Royal William, weighing anchor at six on sighting Russell to the west-ward, was fouled by the 50-gun *Advice* of Rooke's division, and had her sprit topmast carried away. Ashby had stood to the north-westward during the night with the other two divisions, 'judging it to be the properest course to meet with our own fleet and the enemy's in the morning'.[6] By half past four in the morning the wind had died and there was a thick fog, so Ashby and the ships with him anchored for a couple of hours. Then, seeing Delaval's division with all sails set, they weighed, and by nine were with the fleet.

Tourville's fleet, in spite of the damage it had sustained, showed a remarkable cohesion. The admiral had fired a gun as a signal to weigh anchor at one in the morning, but only seven ships sailed in company with him; the other groups had joined forces soon after the morning mist dispersed. At this time he had in fact a total of 34 ships still in company. D'Amfreville and Relingue from the van squadron, who had anchored overnight at some distance from the Dutch, brought a total of 12 ships. Langeron from the white squadron had joined forces with Gabaret and two consorts, and was heading out across the Channel, hoping to reach Brest. Only the little 16-gun *Saudadoes* seems to have had an early morning sight of two of these ships making off, and to have chased them for a while. Villette thought it a bizarre course for Langeron to take, and mentions that Langeron may have been upset by an order signalled before the action to take up his appointed station. French nobles were notoriously touchy, even petty, when they thought that their honour had been impugned.

Villette had his whole division, and nine ships of the centre and rear squadrons, 15 ships in all, in company. He had given them orders to weigh as soon as the ebb began. The movement was well executed: by dawn, aided by the mist, he was out of sight of the allies. But he was also out of touch with Tourville, and remained under easy sail, awaiting news of him. Villette and d'Amfreville joined forces an hour after daylight. They sighted, and ignored, two groups of what they took to be crippled English ships steering north, though one group must have been either Gabaret or Langeron making for mid-Channel. When the sun was strong enough to disperse the mist, Tourville's seven ships came into view, and the whole force of 34 ships came together.

Nesmond, who had not received the order to anchor, had all five ships of his division in company, and had been joined by the *Entendu* from Gabaret's division in the rear. She had somehow found herself separated from everybody else. With these six, which must have drifted clear to the eastward of the anchored ships, Nesmond eluded the allies and headed in for la Hougue.

While the ebb lasted and the wind remained in the east the French main body made good speed along the Norman coast west of Cap Barfleur, the Dutch at their heels and the English in sight. Tourville's feelings can be imagined when at this moment an officer came on board to deliver Pontchartrain's orders to retire in view of the junction of the allied fleets. Another copy of the order was carried by a vessel taken off Cap Barfleur by Wyvil in the *Centurion* as he hastened after the fleet.

By noon the wind had gone round to something south of west, but the tide was still favourable; the French were tacking along the shore; Shovell's division and Ashby's squadron had closed up from astern. The *Hampton Court* and *Sandwich*, with one fireship, were limping back to Spithead. At eight in the morning they had four French ships in sight, no doubt the group attempting to reach Brest by the centre of the Channel. Another English ship in a bad way was the *Montagu*. Her crew had worked all night, knotting and splicing the rigging, and hoisting a temporary main yard, constructed by binding two other spars to what was left of the original yard. At ten the captain sent a lieutenant on board Ashby's flagship, and received permission to leave the fleet and return to the rendezvous at St Helen's. In the afternoon he had the Isle of Wight in sight.

By four in the afternoon the ebb was finished and the wind was still contrary; both fleets lay at anchor in sight of one another, the Dutch having closed the gap to a mile and a half. The *Soleil Royal* had taken in so much water that she would hardly steer, and had been delaying the whole fleet. It is even possible that Tourville might have saved all the rest, had he abandoned his flagship during the previous night. Villette certainly thought so, and made strong personal representations to his commander-in-chief. In case the great three-decker had to be left to her fate, Tourville shifted his flag as night fell by boat to the *Ambitieux*, in which his vice admiral had given him such telling support. The two captains on board the *Soleil Royal* demurred, but were given a direct order to remain with the fleet as a private ship.

The *Royal Catherine*'s captain took advantage of the spell at anchor to re-muster his ship's company, and found that he had lost 15 killed and about 80 wounded. Many ships were busy heeling to stop leaks, getting up new spars and reeving new rigging. The *Kent* and *Ruby*, which had stood to the northward under topsails instead of chasing westward during the night, now found themselves anchored well to leeward of the rest of the fleet, near their rear admiral's flagship, which had been almost disabled by the punishment she had received while drifting between the French ships. Half an hour before midnight Shovell shifted his flag to the *Kent*.

All ships weighed anchor at about this time and resumed the chase westward, tacking along the coast in the favourable tidal stream. The *Eagle* had difficulty in getting her anchor home, so few were her active seamen left, and shortly afterwards the *Britannia*'s fore topmast, damaged in action on the previous day, came down. According to one account, Russell's red squadron shortened sail and stood by the flagship while her crew cleared away the fallen mast and repaired the damage in the darkness, instead of pressing on after the enemy. Though there is no record of any contemporary criticism, they were wrong to do so: the signal for general chase had not been countermanded; the fighting instructions were specific in ordering 'every ship to use its best endeavours to come up with the enemy and lay them on board'.[7] There were only six hours for the fleets to tack along the shore. With the coming of the flood at about four in the morning of 21 May, both fleets were forced to anchor again.

The French had weathered Cap de la Hague, and 21 of them were anchored in the Alderney race; the remaining 13 lay close under the cape. Tourville had decided that his fleet should go through the race. He judged, correctly as it turned out, that the allies would not attempt the passage through these notorious waters, 15 miles of very violent currents with such poor holding ground that vessels in difficulties could seldom save themselves by anchoring. The English and Dutch were a few miles to leeward, and still outside the race, the Dutch and most of the blue squadron closest to the enemy.

At seven the flood was so strong that the 13 enemy ships lying close to the cape began to drag their anchors, and were eventually forced to cut their cables and run eastward before the wind. Most of them had then no anchors left. 'By the Almighty's assistance', as the *Britannia*'s log has it, 'and the strength of the tide', they drove rapidly to leeward. They were quickly clear of the Dutch and blue squadrons, but ships of the red squadron, delayed by the flagship's mishap, were in a better position to take some action. Russell ordered his squadron to cut their cables so as to resume the hunt, but the French were past them all, flying before the stiff breeze with the flood tide under them, before they could move.

Tourville, realizing that he could no longer control the fleet, hauled down his flag on board the *Ambitieux*, and signalled 'sauve qui peut'. Pannetier, still with the ships anchored in the race, hoisted the signal to rally, and has been credited with saving the rest of the fleet, the command of which now devolved upon him as the senior officer present. Of the 11 great ships mounting more than 80 guns with which Tourville had gone into action two days before, only two remained: the *Grand*, Pannetier's flagship, and the *Conquérant*, one of Tourville's seconds. Nesmond in the *Monarque* was at la Hougue, Langeron in the *Souverain* and Gabaret in the *Orgueilleux* were proceeding independently to Brest, and all the rest (the *Soleil Royal*, *Merveilleux*, *Foudroyant*, *Ambitieux*, *Saint-Philippe* and *Admirable*) were with the group running eastward along the coast.

Some of the English blue squadron, including its vice admiral in the *Neptune* and many of his division, cut and followed Russell, giving him about 40 ships, but the majority stayed with Ashby and the Dutch so as to attempt to deal with the 21 French ships still at anchor. The *Ossory* had a boat overturned while trying to get in the masts and sails of her longboat. She had to send her pinnace to rescue the crew of five from the water. She saved them all, 'but it hindered the chase very much'.[8] The *Monk*, anchored in 54 fathoms, had found that her small bower anchor would not hold her. Her best bower had been lost when she had cut her cable on the evening of the fleet action, so she had let go her stream anchor in an effort to stop dragging. She lost both of the anchors down when Russell made the signal to cut, leaving her only her spare anchor in the hold.

At noon Ashby's ships and the Dutch weighed anchor and started tacking to windward, and in the afternoon the 50-gun *Adventure* captured a French fireship which had become detached from the rest of the fleet. At half past five, when the fleets again anchored, the French still had a comfortable lead of about nine miles. The Dutch had been impressed by Tourville's discomfiture in attempting to take great ships through the race, and had decided to sail around Alderney.

There then took place in the French fleet an incident commemorated by Robert Browning in the poem *Hervé Riel*, published in the *Cornhill Magazine* in 1871. None of the local pilots would take the warships through the race. According to Browning's account, which mistakes both the admiral and the flagship, a council of war was held, and a decision taken to run the ships ashore, blow them up or burn them on the beach so as to keep them out of enemy hands. Then there appeared a Breton coasting pilot named Hervé Riel, a native of Croisic at the mouth of the Loire, who had been pressed into the French Royal Navy. He declared that he knew the waters well and could pilot the fleet to safety.

'Only let me lead the line,
Make the others follow mine.'

The admiral agreed. When therefore the fleets weighed anchor again on the ebb an hour before midnight, the French successfully stood south through the race to reach harbour and safety at St Malo. Russell heard over a month later that one of them, probably the *Conquérant*, arrived with nine feet of water in her hold and over 200 casualties. Asked to name his reward, Riel said that he would like leave to return to his wife Aurore at Croisic. 'That he got and nothing more.'

The allies too stood to windward during the night, but when daylight came the enemy fleet was no longer in sight from Ashby's flagship. The wind was fresh at a little south of west, and Ashby's pilot was not 'willing to venture amongst the islands'.[9] At half past five the Dutch, evidently considering they could do no more, bore eastward after Russell. They had taken a French fireship sheltering at Alderney.

It might have been different had Carter been alive. He had passed through the race in the opposite direction in a 3rd-rate, the *Montagu*, only three weeks earlier. But Carter had died of his wounds on the previous day, and the *Montagu* had retired to refit. Benbow, who had visited St Malo several times in merchant vessels, might have been prepared to pilot the fleet, or at least the 3rd rates and smaller ships, through the race. But Benbow had scudded away eastward on board the fleet flagship, which also carried a Jersey pilot. There is no evidence that any commanding officer or master, who had shared the experience in Carter's squadron, offered Ashby any advice in favour of risking the passage, or that the admiral considered shifting his flag to a 3rd-rate in order to maintain the pursuit. Of course there is a vast difference between making the passage northbound with a favourable wind and tide, popping out into the open waters of the Channel, like a cork out of a bottle, and the reverse passage, heading for unknown rocks and shoals, propelled forward by the wind and a fearsome tidal stream.

There was of course another option open to Ashby: he could keep up the chase by making the longer passage round the Caskets. Russell later condemned him and Almonde most bitterly for not doing so. ''Twas a great error,' he wrote, 'for they knew we had no occasion for them with us.'[10] Some of Ashby's ships, and the *Lennox* of Delaval's division, had anchored north-west of the Caskets during the night of 21/22 May, and at daylight were between nine and 12 miles north of Guernsey, still in sight of the French fleet, which had spent the night close under the island. It is true that the allies were not making any ground, and could not now catch the enemy before they reached harbour. They had seen the French weather the island of Guernsey and bear up for St Malo, and knew that they could not themselves weather it until the next tide. There can be little doubt, however, that a resolute pursuit, using the enemy to lead through the dangers of rock and shoal, would have occasioned further losses among the French as they crowded into the narrow entrance of St Malo. Their crews were thoroughly demoralized, and could not have been expected to make much resistance. A fortnight later Russell confessed that he could not sleep 'for thinking of the stupidity which lost the French fleet'.[11]

Half an hour after the Dutch had gone, the ships of the blue squadron bore away to the eastward. Those ahead of them had already been busy.

Chapter 7

Van Dienst: the Hogue. The French ships burning would have been beached broadside on and would have had their sails furled (The National Maritime Museum, London).

Kill   *22-24 May 1692*

At about eleven o'clock on the morning of 21 May, as the flying French squadron came opposite Cherbourg, three ships were seen to detach themselves, come up into the wind, and start to beat to windward along the shore. The tide had just turned, so that they had the ebb under their lee bows, forcing them westward again, but the manoeuvre was a forlorn hope, the last effort of a tired and distracted quarry. The English warships, like a pack of hounds closing round a stag at bay, were too close to permit any escape. Cherbourg had no harbour worth the name, and puny fortifications. Earlier it had been better defended, but Vauban's works had been demolished on the orders of Louvois when Minister of War, allegedly to spite the Minister of Marine. The *Soleil Royal* beached herself under the guns of a six-gun fort in the fosse du Galet, cut away her masts, and lay there to await her fate. The *Triomphant* and *Admirable* were also run ashore, one near the protection of two coastal towers, the other to the east of the town. With them were two small frigates and a fireship.

Shovell in the *Kent*, with his former flagship the *Royal William* in company, met the French opposite Cherbourg as he laboured westward, and was soon leading the chase of the other ten, occasionally coming within gunshot, but withholding his fire. Russell, not far astern, held on also, ordering Delaval, towards the rear of the chasing ships, to keep enough force to destroy the enemy ships ashore, and to send on the rest. Sir Ralph found that he had far too large a detachment at his disposal. By mid-afternoon no fewer than 27 English ships had anchored or were lying off the shore so as to be in at the kill. He ordered 16 of them to resume the chase eastward.

Delaval's first attempt to approach the stranded ships was repelled. Ships sent in to sound the depth of water in the approaches were greeted with shots from the fort. Shifting his flag to the 50-gun *St Albans* of Shovell's division, and taking the *Ruby* and two fireships, Delaval stood in towards the shore, leaving the bigger ships and other 4th-rates further out. The attacking vessels attracted heavy fire from the enemy. Anchored in four fathoms of water the little 4th-rates kept up their firing for an hour and a half at the ships and the fort. 'They galled me so extremely', Sir Ralph admitted in his despatch, that he retreated out of range and anchored for the night.[1]

Next morning, 22 May, Delaval sent the *St Albans* and *Advice* to anchor near the shore and fire at the exposed bottom of the *Admirable*, heeling towards the shore. They were engaged by the other two French ships but came to little harm, though the *Advice* had two guns dismounted by shot. Delaval himself, with his flag in the 70-gun *Grafton*, anchored in seven fathoms to batter the enemy, but there was insufficient depth of water to deploy the rest of the ships of the 3rd and 4th rates which, with the *Monk* leading, had been ordered to stand in nearer to the enemy.

Delaval therefore decided to send in three fireships in an attempt to finish off the enemy, following them up himself with all the serviceable boats he could muster. He had shifted his flag again, this time to the *Burford*, and he waited on board her till high water an hour after noon before launching the assault with a handsome breeze just north of west. 'Our fireships came very boldly on,' wrote the master of the *Advice* after observing the attack from his ringside position, 'notwithstanding the French plied their guns to admiration upon them.'

The fireship *Blaze*, commanded by Thomas Heath, steered for the westernmost enemy ship, the *Soleil Royal*. Her three masts protruded to seaward from her hull, protecting her side, and she had boats out for the same purpose. Abandoned when within pistol shot, the *Blaze*, by a measure of good fortune as well as skill, lay athwart the stern of the former French fleet flagship, and soon engulfed her in flames. The beautifully carved and decorated stern with its great cabin, in which the fateful decision to fight had been taken, and in which, according to reports later circulating in London, were representations of Louis XIV with the kings and princes of Europe in chains at his feet, made good firewood. Later the stricken ship was shattered by an explosion.

James Greenway was able to place his fireship the *Wolf* alongside the *Triomphant*, and she too was burnt to the waterline. Many contemporary accounts, including Delaval's despatch, though not the *Royal Sovereign*'s log, list this victim as the *Conquérant* owing to double translation of the name, but that ship, as already related, had been amongst those which had escaped to St Malo.

The third fireship, the *Hound*, was set on fire by enemy shot as she approached, and had to be run aground and abandoned. Delaval therefore took the boats to destroy the remaining enemy ship. Her crew could make little resistance because she lay so much on her side. Seeing the fate of their two consorts, they hauled down her colours and made haste to escape from her disengaged side. Beaujeu was the last officer to leave his ship, where only about 40 men, most of them wounded, remained. On the vice admiral's orders, all these men were made prisoners and removed before the ship was set on fire. He thought it necessary to apologize to Nottingham for having taken these prisoners; he would have landed them on their own shore had he not sighted sails in the offing and feared an attack by a fresh enemy force. The strange sails turned out to belong to the ships with Ashby and Almonde, baulked of their prey off Alderney, and rejoining the flag.

Delaval wrote a report of his proceedings for Nottingham, and detached the *Ruby* to take it to Portsmouth. He also sent off the *Fubbs* yacht to find and report to Russell. The commander-in-chief showed considerable resentment that his vice admiral should have reported direct to the Secretary of State in this fashion. Strictly Delaval should not have done so, but the admiral was wrong to reprove him. Delaval had scored a great success, Russell had disappeared eastward in pursuit of the French remnant, and the junior flag officer could not know that he would find his admiral next day at anchor off la Hougue, only a few miles along the coast. In these circumstances he would have been open to serious criticism from Whitehall had he sent no report, and failed to find the commander-in-chief within a few days. His force destroyed, besides the three large ships at Cherbourg, two small frigates of 24 and 20 guns, and a fireship.

Delaval's ships stood out to join Ashby's and the Dutch at four in the afternoon, but they all had to come to an anchor four hours later when the flood started making. The *Captain* collided with the *Bonaventure* on anchoring, and carried away her bowsprit. As the sun went down the smoke at Cherbourg, 'three great smokes' as one log records, could be plainly seen 18 miles away. Next day Delaval rounded Cap Barfleur and came to anchor off la Hougue soon after noon on 23 May, close to the remainder of the English fleet. His ships, and Ashby's, were now in time to witness and to play a part in the final act of the drama. Although Almonde offered Dutch assistance, Russell had plenty of force available from the red and blue squadrons for what he had in mind.

As Shovell rounded Cap Barfleur on the evening of 21 May he could see a small group of enemy ships bearing away to the eastward. Danby saw them too, in the last of the daylight, after he had anchored east of the cape. He counted six sail, some of them with jury topmasts, as he examined them through his perspective glass, an early form of telescope. They were making all the sail they could to the eastward. This was Nesmond's contingent, now four ships of the line and two attendant vessels, for he had left behind two others, the *Bourbon* and *Saint-Louis*, which had rallied to the larger French force on its arrival. He meant to run up the Channel, pass through the straits of Dover, and circumnavigate the British Isles northabout, as the Spanish armada had done 104 years before. He had to leave two more ships at le Havre, but the other two, though sighted off Beachy Head on 27 May, reached Brest safely after a final chase some time much later. It was over three months before the English received word that the *Entendu* had broken her back and sunk at le Havre.

Shovell had followed the other ten French ships to the roadstead of la Hougue. Only the *Cambridge* was with him, the rest, except the *Resolution*, which came up soon afterwards, being at least six miles astern. They were not, however, alone in the approaches to the anchorage. The *Cambridge* took a French sloop of 15 guns and, after Shovell had anchored at ten at night, his barge went away and sank a French coasting shallop laden with honey and butter.

Russell too had anchored his flagship at ten at night, but a good deal further out than Shovell in the *Kent*. At four next morning, 22 May, he weighed and stood in, but was forced to drop anchor again when the tide turned against him. All 12 French ships, two of Nesmond's and the ten more recent arrivals, were clearly in view, warped close to the shore of the bay, one of them, the *Terrible*, aground on the ledge of rocks that forms the island of Tatihou off the coast, and listing on her side, though she had been shored up by her crew. All the rest had their topmasts and yards struck, and were aground at low water. Their crews had made use of the yards and other spars as shores to keep the ships upright so that the guns could still be fired.

The ships were grouped in sixes, half given some protection by the guns of the Fort de l'Ilet near the spot where the *Terrible* lay, and the remainder opposite the town and the fort of St Vaast, over which flew, beside the white flag of France, a flag bearing the crosses of St George and St Andrew to denote the presence of King James, whose army was encamped round the village of Morsalines to the southwestward.

Berwick, whose younger brother Henry Fitzjames was serving on board one of the French warships in Tourville's fleet, records that the men of the waiting army had heard the sounds of the naval battle very distinctly. When, next morning, French ships started arriving they were at first thought to form part of the victorious fleet coming to transport them to England. These must have been Nesmond's ships. Tourville's remnant came in a day and a half later, and the English fleet could soon afterwards be seen assembling in the offing, powerfully reinforced when Delaval arrived, followed by Ashby and the Dutch under Almonde.

Tourville, accompanied by d'Amfreville and Villette, immediately reported to James for orders. A council was called, attended by Marshal Bellefonds and Bonrepaus of the invasion committee, Nicolas Foucault, the Intendant of Normandy, and all flag and general officers present. It was resolved to defend the ships if attacked; James and Tourville were agreed that it would contribute neither to the glory of King Louis, nor to the honour of the French nation, if the ships were to be run ashore. Foucault at once sent for all the powder in two magazines in Normandy. The ships were short of it; moreover their captains reported that what they had was little better than charcoal; the enemy's powder sent each

shot half as far again as theirs. When Foucault reported to the marshal
that the powder had arrived, he was surprised to be told that the plan
had been changed; it had been decided to run the ships aground after
taking off as much of their stores and armaments as was possible, and to
try by means of boats to frustrate any attempt by the English to burn
them. Additional gun platforms were to be set up on the shores of the
bay, but James's suggestion that troops should be put on board the
ships, so as to repel such an attempt, was not accepted. Had it been
adopted the outcome might not have been different; but at least the
English would have been made to pay more dearly for their success.

It is evident that there was considerable confusion in the councils of
the French high command. News of Pannetier's safe arrival at St Malo
had been received, but a report from Cherbourg, that several officers and
men had been blown up with their ship, was sufficient to start a new
panic at la Hougue. Villette went to James, at the marshal's request, to
say that the crews must be withdrawn.

The English granted the enemy a respite of almost two days. After
calling commanding officers together during the early evening of 22
May, Russell gave orders for Shovell in the *Kent* to take the 3rd and 4th
rates, frigates and fireships to destroy the French ships. The first
requirement was to know whether there was sufficient depth of water to
reach a fighting range. Russell therefore ordered the little 16-gun
Greyhound to stand towards the shore and sound. At six fathoms she was
to brail up her mainsail, and at five fathoms she was to come off again. In
the event she stood in till she was within musket shot of the enemy
ships, and still had 7½ fathoms of water when she started back to report.
In order to prevent any chance of escape during the night, the 4th rates
were told to anchor in a line close inshore, the 3rd rates further out, and
those of the first two rates further out still. All these great ships anchored
near the *Britannia* were instructed to prepare to man and arm their
pinnaces and barges, and to send them to the *Kent* when ordered.
During the same evening the *Fubbs* yacht arrived with Delaval's report of
his success at Cherbourg and the earlier capture of a French fireship by
the blue squadron. Russell sent the yacht back to Delaval with instructions to send all available fireships to la Hougue.

At six next morning Shovell ordered the inshore squadron to weigh,
and gave them a line of battle for going in to the attack (see Appendix 4),
but there was little or no wind, and they were forced to anchor soon after
noon. In spite of the precautions taken, two enemy privateers had come
out of la Hougue; the *Greyhound* was sent to chase them, but they
escaped into a neighbouring harbour.

Shovell, who had been wounded during the fleet action by a splinter
in the thigh, then reported that he was suffering from a sudden and
severe indisposition, which was probably due to blood poisoning, and

that he was unable to carry out his orders. On hearing of it, Rooke immediately sought the admiral's leave to take Shovell's place, and was directed to do so. Shovell's flag was struck on board the *Kent* and rehoisted when he was carried back to the *Royal William*. Rooke too shifted his flag, from the *Neptune* to the *Eagle*, and at three in the afternoon ordered all longboats, barges and pinnaces to muster alongside her.

Danby had been up since four, and had been rowed over to the *Kent*, with his barge and longboat manned and armed, in order to accompany Sir Cloudisley as a volunteer in the fight. Learning of the vice admiral's relinquishment of the command, he went on board the *Woolwich* to dine with Myngs, and at four in the afternoon set out with Myngs in his barge with a lead and line to take soundings. They came under fire, but persisted in their self-imposed task for over an hour, when Aylmer arrived in his boat to tell them of Rooke's appointment. They all three went on board the *Eagle*, which was already standing in towards the shore, to report their findings. Rooke had already issued his orders verbally to the commanding officers of the small ships and the lieutenants of the boats, and he now placed Danby and another captain in general charge of the boats and fireships. Then he anchored in six fathoms. His force contained 14 ships of the 3rd and 4th rates, with six smaller vessels and eight fireships (see Appendix 4).

After a preliminary bombardment lasting an hour by the guns of this squadron, Rooke made a weft with his ensign which was the signal to send the boats in with the tide against the northern group of enemy ships. This group contained four great ships of between 96 and 82 guns, the *Ambitieux*, *Merveilleux*, *Saint-Philippe* and *Foudroyant*. The other two mounted 76 guns; one was the *Magnifique*, and the other the *Terrible*, still almost overset on the island of Tatihou which lies off the town and can be reached by foot at low tide. It was said afterwards that James had dined on board the *Saint-Philippe*.

At about half past eight a captain of one of the expended fireships managed to board the easiest target, the wrecked *Terrible*, and to set her on fire, and half an hour later the rest of the boats moved forward on the other five. They were met with a hail of musket shot from the ports of the warships in addition to cannon fire from the fort, and for a time were unable to advance. Danby therefore ordered ten of the boats to tow the nearest fireship, the *Thomas and Elizabeth*, towards the enemy, drawing the bulk of the fire, though one cannon ball passed through Danby's barge, tearing his stocking and grazing his leg. He and the crew managed to scramble out of the stern of the boat into another as she sank.

The *Tiger* prize, of 42 guns, continued to exchange shots with the fort as the boats approached the doomed ships. The French had not had time to protect their temporary gun platforms with earthworks, and the

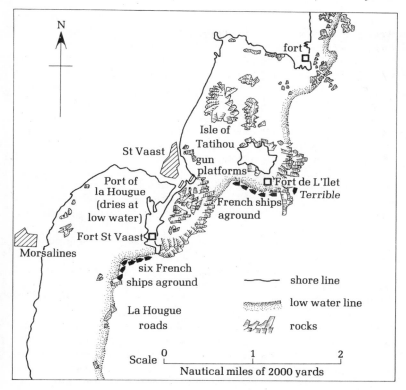

Map 7. La Hougue: 23 and 24 May: French ships and defences.
(The positions of the gun platforms are conjectural.)

gunners had already deserted these exposed positions. The few seamen left on board the battleships, exhorted to sell their lives dearly, intimated that they had already had enough fighting, and began to leave their posts.

The French boats, which numbered only a dozen and in which Tourville and other senior officers had embarked, made no difference to the result. Sèbeville, captain of the *Terrible*, who had stranded his ship in what the French termed a very lubberly manner on his arrival, was wounded in the encounter. Berwick observes laconically that the English, 'more accustomed and handy than our people at this kind of manoeuvre', repelled them and forced them ashore again.[2] Stephen Martin, the lieutenant in charge of one of the *Eagle*'s boats, found himself aground and under attack from troops from the shore. In a rare, but not unique, encounter between the Royal Navy and enemy cavalry, a trooper was pulled off his horse by the bowman's boathook. Martin's men successfully refloated the boat and resumed their work.

The English boats' crews, some of whom had provided themselves with fireworks from the fireships, climbed up the sides of the enemy ships, only two of which were afloat. Ignoring any Frenchmen who might still be on board, they set about burning the ships. The *Centurion*'s boat's crew found a three-decker completely deserted; they quickly cut chips of wood for kindling. A rapid inspection of one of the great ships showed Danby that all her guns on the landward side were loaded. Those in the lower tier were housed, but many of those on the upper and middle gundecks were pointing at the fort. He made his men train the rest round to point at it, so that the ship would 'do execution upon her own fort' when she was on fire. Then on his knees blowing hemp and oakum to start a blaze, he had his face burnt when some loose gunpowder caught fire near by.

French resistance was in fact remarkably feeble after the approach of the English fireship. They had available more than 200 boats and three small oared frigates, each mounting 12 guns, but promises to use them for defence were not fulfilled. If these craft had been manned and armed, if the ships' guns had been used as well as the batteries ashore and the muskets afloat, and if the crews had been reinforced with soldiers, the English boats might well have suffered a repulse and the fireships have been warded off. But Villette had successfully evacuated most of the crews, and had even started to set fire to three ships before his orders were countermanded. Confusion appears to have been allowed to reign, while the king and the marshal looked on, as if at a display of fireworks, and Bonrepaus sat unconcernedly in his room. The soldiers had not even been issued with powder and ball. Had the English wished to take possession of Tatihou, they could easily have done so.

When the tide turned all the English boats withdrew by the light of the burning ships, towing the fireship, which had not been needed, though it had been placed alongside two enemy ships before it was seen that the boats' crews could do all that was necessary to accomplish their destruction. Danby was full of praise for the fireship captain's restraint in accepting orders not to carry out the work his ship existed to fulfil. An hour before midnight there was a heavy explosion as an enemy magazine blew up. Some boats reached their parent vessels after midnight; the crews of others were told to remain with the inshore squadron for the night. The six enemy ships had been destroyed at negligible loss.

The boats' crews were not given much rest. Rooke and Danby, boarding the *Chester* late at night, gave orders that the boats should report alongside that ship in the morning. And at five on the morning of 24 May the signal was made for them to muster again so that they could be sent in on the next tide against the remaining French ships at the opposite end of the bay, protected by a rather stronger battery in the fort of St Vaast. According to prisoners it had 68 guns mounted, compared with 44 in the outer fort.

At eight the bombardment began from the *Deptford* and *Crown*, with the *Charles* galley and the *Greyhound* in support. The wind, near south-easterly, was favourable. The English boats, advancing in good order with the brigantine under oars as a half-galley, ran alongside the enemy ships, evoking a much-quoted favourable comment from their former Lord High Admiral, a comment that can hardly have endeared him to the staff around him. 'Ah!' the king is reported to have exclaimed, 'none but my brave English could do so brave an action!'[3] None of the Stuarts was strong on tact; James lacked it to a remarkable degree.

The French troops lining the shore were as demoralized as the seamen. They could scarcely be induced to stand to arms behind the parapets of the fortifications at St Vaast and on Tatihou. They wasted their ammunition by blazing away at the English boats before they came within range. Nevertheless it was a considerable fusillade from the fort and shore that the boats had withstood.

The English seamen started fires on board the enemy ships as on the previous evening. They also engaged the French platforms with some of the ships' guns, and one ball passed close to James as he watched from the shore. This attack accounted for two 76-gun ships, the *Fier* and *Tonnant*, and four more, the *Gaillard*, *Bourbon*, *Saint-Louis* and *Fort*, mounting between 68 and 60 guns. A French frigate or fireship was also burnt; the destruction of this vessel provides the reason for the discrepancies between the different accounts of the action. Most English accounts, by including it, claim a total of 13 enemy ships destroyed, while the French admit only the 12 previously in the line at Barfleur.

The boats lay off on their oars for about an hour in order to avoid any danger if one or more of the burning ships were to blow up. Danby, returning from the blazing ships, was hailed by Rooke, afloat in his barge, and asked whether he thought it was possible to burn the transport ships lying inside the harbour. 'Ay!' he called back. 'It can be safely done, for now I believe our men will do anything!'

Rooke therefore ordered some boats to tow in two fireships, and then, his vice admiral's flag flying in the bows of his barge, passed the word for the boats to follow him into the harbour. It was no easy matter to board the transports, with small shot coming from them as well as from both sides of the narrow harbour. Again it was the captain of an expended fireship who managed, in spite of a throat wound, to get on board one and to start a fire. This had the effect of clearing the enemy out of the neighbouring vessels, so that they too were burnt, together with a warship, equivalent in size to an English 4th- or 5th-rate, lying alongside a hulk.

Both fireships had run aground close under the fort. There was no possibility of getting them off, so they were fired by their own crews. When one exploded it cast burning debris into the fort of St Vaast, causing an explosion there just as the boats were withdrawing from the harbour, bringing with them a few captured small craft. The tide had turned once more, helping the boats to return to the fleet, many of them showing in their bows the French colours they had captured, and most carrying personal booty taken by the men.

Losses, though heavier than on the previous night, were still very small. The *London*'s longboat was lost and her crew wounded, the *Victory*'s boats had three men wounded, the *Vanguard*'s pinnace left two men behind on board a French warship, and her longboat had one man wounded. The *Elizabeth* had nine casualties from small shot. Total deaths were about ten, and there were some accidental injuries.

The wind was still easterly, and the boats gave some assistance to the frigates to get clear of the fort. The *Oxford* had to send away two warps before she could make sail from her anchorage off the town. Rooke, after examining two prisoners taken the night before, sailed the inshore squadron back to the fleet anchorage and, his mission completed, shifted his flag back to the *Neptune*.

No English or French account mentions any Dutch participation in this final stage of the action. A Dutch historian says that admirals Almonde and Schey, as well as Schryver, captain of the *Zeeland*, all reported that the Dutch helped, though he finds it curious that none of them gave any details.[4] There is, strangely enough, a print of the Hogue by an English artist showing a boat with a Dutch flag taking part in the attack on the enemy ships.

Rooke had not completed the destruction of the shipping in the harbour. Vessels at the top of it were high and dry, and it did not seem sensible to expose the men to the inevitable casualties of a landing in face of trained and well-armed troops, for two fresh regiments had marched down from the camp and were lining the shore. There were not in any event so many transports as had been expected for so large an expeditionary force. Russell wrote afterwards that there were not more than 20 or 30 three-masted vessels and some open boats.

During the afternoon Russell sent in under a flag of truce a boat carrying some of the prisoners who had been brought off to the fleet. He not only wished to land the prisoners, but hoped to discover the names of the ships he had destroyed. The French, incensed at the display of white flags shown by the victorious English boats earlier in the day, took this new approach as a further insult, and opened fire.

Another French prisoner was wounded, and was sent to join the worst English casualties on board the hospital ship *Concord*. As soon as Russell had completed his reports for Nottingham and the Admiralty, he despatched the 50-gun *Bonaventure* to escort the hospital ship to England, and to send his letters to their destinations by express. They sailed at five, and reached Spithead at half past two next afternoon, after holding a direct course with an easterly wind. The admiral made a point of asking Nottingham not to publish his report. It was not written in a form fit for publication. It was meant for the queen, and he did not want it exposed in every coffee house.

The admiral's next task was to direct that public prayers and thanksgiving, according to the liturgy of the Church of England, should be said 'with all possible devotion' throughout the fleet on the following Friday, 27 May. Finally he sent Ashby to le Havre with 12 English and as many Dutch warships under Callenburg, and three fireships, with orders to destroy any shipping there and, if this should prove impossible, to return to St Helen's. At eight in the evening the rest of the fleet weighed their anchors and stood out of the bay for the Isle of Wight.

This was one occasion on which Russell appears to have over-ruled the decisions reached at a council of war. According to Almonde's despatch, it was decided that an allied fleet of 50 or 60 ships, including the largest, should proceed to Ushant in order to take any enemy vessels that might appear off Brest, and that the rest should scour the coast of France as far as Dunkirk, so as to seek out and destroy the remnant of the French fleet that had gone eastward. By returning directly to England, Russell lost any chance of intercepting the four damaged French ships struggling down Channel, but he probably saved the allies from serious losses by storm damage when the weather changed shortly afterwards.

At noon next day, as the last stragglers of the allied fleet were clearing the anchorage, a boat came off from the shore under a flag of truce carrying a Scots Jacobite and a French flag officer who may have been Relingue. They brought a letter from Tourville seeking to excuse the rudeness of the fort in firing at the boat sent in by Russell under a flag of truce. They said that a present of wine had been prepared for the victorious admiral, but they did not bring it in the boat, and Russell, well out in the Channel, knew nothing of the incident till a couple of days later.

Other thoughts had been troubling him. On the day after the action off Barfleur he had received fresh orders from the queen and a covering letter from Nottingham. We can detect here the first sign of his impatience with arm-chair strategists in Whitehall giving orders which he knew to be unsound. For the queen's letter showed a distrust of the decision reached by a council of war at St Helen's on 15 May. She urged him, in particularly woolly terms, to divide his forces by sending a force across to Normandy to guard against invasion and taking the main fleet to the westward so as to counter the threat posed by the French fleet off the Dorset coast. Russell, however, could see that Tourville posed no threat to England until he had joined the transports reported to be assembled at la Hougue. Tourville's appearance off the English coast had been caused by the weather; if the wind had been favourable he would have reached la Hougue before the allied fleet sailed. Russell's appreciation had been amply vindicated by events. By steering straight for the point of danger he had made Tourville's mission impossible of achievement.

Always quick to take offence, the admiral saw in the queen's letter a reflection on his diligence in joining the fleet and his despatch in sailing from St Helen's. He knew that such opinions had been expressed in London, and he felt aggrieved that the government should encourage them. Anchored in la Hougue roads, the final destruction of the enemy delegated to a junior flag officer, he had brooded over the two letters and had become more and more agitated and morose at the injustice to his reputation and lack of confidence in his judgment that they appeared to show. Although he had just forced the French fleet to flee, abandoning its mission of escorting an invasion flotilla, and although his forces had destroyed three large enemy warships off Cherbourg and now had 12 more at their mercy, he was quite ready to go home and live quietly without the fatigue of caring for the fleet; there were plenty of others better qualified than he. In a despairing letter to Nottingham giving vent to these feelings from a full head and heart, he urged the Secretary of State to employ some one else. He did not care whom, so long as the admiral chosen was not a Jacobite. It was typical of the man that he could not omit a reference to his finances, pointing out that he was considerably worse off than when William had come to England.[5]

Russell is seen at his worst in this letter. He could not bear any criticism, direct or implied, of his conduct of the fleet's operations. By any standard he had done well, and had saved the country. Within 24 hours of his committing these thoughts to paper, his fleet had completed the greatest naval victory in the history of England up to that time. Instead of letting his achievements speak for themselves, he felt obliged to complain. It may be argued in his defence that he could foresee the troubles ahead if the queen in council continued to be given advice at variance with the opinion of those who would have the job of carrying out her orders. Events were to justify this forecast of differences between the Government and its commanders at sea, but it is difficult to avoid the conclusion that Russell's attitude to authority made a substantial contribution to all the difficulties that were to arise. It can also be said that, with the speed of communications limited to those of the horse and the sailing despatch boat, some instructions were bound to be out of date by the time they were received. It would have been possible for Russell to ignore the queen's orders, since they had been overtaken by events. As a politician he cared too much for principle to be able to do so. He might have been a great admiral, remembered by later generations, if the politician in him had not kept breaking through.

Highly exaggerated accounts of the fleet action off Cap Barfleur on 19 May were already circulating in the English capital. Russell's first despatch, itself over-optimistic about the results of the encounter, reached Whitehall at four on the morning of Saturday, 21 May. It was followed at noon by another express from Portsmouth, announcing the safe arrival of the Straits and Bilbao convoys. Their escorts 'heard a great shooting at sea, and putting the merchants into port took out of them the ablest seamen, and so sailed with a brisk wind to share in the action'.[6] Then reports began to come in from the disabled ships which were beginning to reach harbour – first the *Montagu*, followed by the *Sandwich* with Hastings' dead body, the *Hampton Court* with Graydon wounded, and the *Zeven Provincien* of the Dutch squadron.

On 24 May, when Nottingham wrote to the king in the Netherlands, he had no news from Russell later than his initial report, but he was able to forward a copy of Almonde's first report to the States-General, another copy of which had been sent to Portland. Nottingham specu-lated that 'we may reasonably expect to hear of greater losses of the French'.[7] He was able to confirm, from the accounts given by the cap-tains of ships already at Spithead, that the allied fleet had suffered no loss. As he was writing, Mees of the *Ruby* brought him Delaval's despatch from Cherbourg with definite news of the destruction of three large enemy warships, and he had it copied for the king. He then went on to quote what Mees told him of the intelligence gained from the captain of the French fireship taken by the *Adventure* off Cap de la Hague. According to this man the French had lost five ships in the fleet action, one being sunk and the others blown up; one of them was Gabaret's flagship. This entirely erroneous information led Nottingham to forecast a total French loss as high as 23; the four enemy warships seen off the Isle of Wight might be caught in addition.

In the event there were to be no further successes, and the final total stood at 16 ships of the line, three at Cherbourg and 12 at la Hougue, with one at le Havre remaining unknown for the next three months. The four in the Channel were sighted and reported a couple of days later between Portland and the Start 'tiding gently down the stream',[8] but no serious attempt seems to have been made to intercept them. There were per-sistent reports during the next three weeks that seven French warships had been lost in the Alderney race, and they were even confirmed by Russell on 12 June on the strength of the testimony of a French fisher-man taken by the *Chester*. It was true that some small French vessels had been driven ashore, but none of them formed part of Tourville's battle fleet.

London went mad with joy as the news of the victory became

generally known. Church bells peeled all day, bonfires glowed by night. Queen Mary, practical as ever, thought first of the wounded. Forty additional surgeons were sent to Portsmouth, and space was cleared in the hospitals of St Thomas at Lambeth and St Bartholomew at Smithfield. For the longer term she gave directions that, as a memorial to the victory, a hospital was to be built for seamen like that already in existence at Chelsea for soldiers. Then she ordered three of her council to Portsmouth with the promise of a large sum of money to be distributed to the seamen who had taken part, and of gold medals for the officers who had distinguished themselves. She did not, however, give instructions for public thanksgiving in the churches, because she hoped shortly to receive equally good news of a land battle in the Low Countries. In this she was disappointed, and later reproached herself bitterly for her pride.

On board the ships of the fleet on 27 May Russell's orders were faithfully obeyed. The assembled crews could more readily appreciate the real significance of the familiar words of the prayer appointed to be used every day in the Royal Navy: 'that we may be a safeguard unto our most gracious Sovereign Lord and Lady, King William and Queen Mary, and their dominions, and a security for such as pass on the seas upon their lawful occasions; that the inhabitants of our Island may in peace and quietness serve thee our God'. And then the thanksgiving after victory: 'The Lord hath wrought a mighty salvation for us. We got not this by our own sword, neither was it our own arm that saved us.'

Evelyn, who had on Trinity Sunday listened to a sermon at Greenwich in which members of the congregation were exhorted to cast their cares on the Providence of God, each doing his own duty, heard within a day or two that 'after all our apprehensions of being invaded, and doubts of our success by sea,' it had 'pleased Almighty God to give us such a victory at sea, to the utter ruin of the French fleet, admiral and all their best men-of-war, transport ships &c., as perhaps never was greater in this part of the world.'[9]

Hastings of the *Sandwich* was given an impressive funeral in London, a regiment of foot marching in front of the hearse, and many coaches following behind, as the procession moved to St James's church in Piccadilly. Carter was buried at Portsmouth, and his widow was granted a yearly pension of £200. As his remains were rowed ashore on 3 June, his former flagship the *Duke*, the *Britannia* and the *Victory* all fired gun salutes, as did the ships of his division.

The writers of songs and ballads were soon busy, turning out doggerel verse of a markedly anti-papist nature, extolling the admirals and the captains of the fireships. Russell's earlier failure to please the mob was forgotten; now he could 'never enough be praised'. The action was described as far greater than that of Lepanto, a manifest exaggeration, as was another couplet asserting that it excelled the Spanish invasion. One ballad was nearer the truth when it declared:

'Twas in eighty-eight Queen Bess swept the main,
In ninety-two Queen Mary the same. [10]

King William of course became William the Conqueror, particularly as bonfires had been lit on the Norman coast. In other respects, and particularly in their predictions, the ballad writers were very wide of the mark.

One asserted that our admirals had scared 'old Lewis' and shaken his throne. But the French king was as secure as ever. He received Tourville kindly, admitted his own responsibility for the naval defeat, and ordered the invasion troops to march to reinforce the armies on the frontiers, the French to Flanders and the Irish to Spain. Before June was out, and before these moves could have any effect, his army in the Netherlands, which had listened to the salutes from the allied camp in celebration of the naval victory, took the great fortress of Namur. It went on to repel an attack by the allied armies at the battle of Steinkirk at the end of July, a bloody fight which neither side won, though the French claimed a victory, and the allies declared that it had saved Liège from sharing the fate of Namur. At the end of the summer Louis, though still surrounded by foes, was no less master of Europe than at the conclusion of any previous campaign.

Another ballad asserted:

Our London merchants will now live at ease
May trade without convoy all over the seas. [11]

On the contrary, the English were now to learn, as France unleashed the *guerre de course*, specifically directed against their merchant shipping, that there is more to the so-called command of the sea than defeating the enemy battle fleet. Her merchants were about to undergo an anxious time, accompanied by heavy losses, and would be all too eager for convoy.

Across the Channel the effect on James was shattering. He was inconsolable, he wrote to his brother king, to have been the cause of such great losses to the French fleet. He no longer deserved the help of so great a monarch, he went on, and prayed His Majesty no longer to interest himself in so unlucky a prince as he. He asked only to be allowed to retire with his family to some corner where he would not interrupt the course of Louis' prosperity and conquests. He returned to St Germains, where his queen gave birth to a daughter shortly afterwards, unattended by anyone of consequence in the government of England or Scotland. James's son Berwick, being younger, accepted the naval catastrophe with a greater show of resilience. Describing it as but an unhappy adventure, he took the road to Flanders, reaching the army there just after its capture of Namur.

Though the intrigues and plotting continued, and there was to be one more scare of invasion in 1696, the Jacobite cause presented no real threat to the Crown for a generation. The discovery and frustration of Grandval's plot to assassinate William in the Netherlands had simultaneously rallied support to the new régime. The War of the League of Augsburg would continue for several years, but the War of the English Succession had been won on the coast of Normandy. Had the allied fleet been a fortnight later in concentrating, Tourville could and would have brushed aside Delaval and Carter, and would have landed James and his Franco-Irish army on the English coast. How much support the 'rightful King' would have received from the Jacobite underground, how quickly the French, and, more particularly, the Irish would have alienated indigenous sympathy, whether the invading army could achieve a decisive result with its communications severed, as must soon have occurred – all these are questions which might have required historical answers.

Just as there had been near panic on the English channel coast two years earlier, so now there was of course considerable consternation on the northern coast of France. D'Estrées and Château-Renault remained firmly in harbour, to be joined by the small forces that reached Brest in safety, either by the Channel route or round the British Isles. Pannetier, his ships warped well away from the sea, was for the present unable to leave St Malo.

Portsmouth dockyard was demonstrating the efficiency of the naval administration in repairing and refitting ships damaged in action. Pepys, so largely responsible for building up this shore support for the fleet, was told that the *Royal William*, sent in by Shovell after the action as unable to keep the sea until repaired, had an inconsiderable number of shot in her sides and masts compared with what she had endured at Solebay when named the *Prince* and serving as flagship of James, Duke of York. This criticism may or may not have had substance, but the *Royal William* was sent away to Chatham for repairs, and was not employed again that summer.

The speed with which other ships were again made seaworthy was remarkable. The early arrivals fared best: the *Hampton Court* had two new topmasts fitted on 23 May, the day on which the *Sandwich* reached St Helen's; she rejoined the fleet before it reached the anchorage; the *Montagu* was quickly repaired and was also again at sea on 25 May. The *Chester* had arrived in a leaking condition, and her crew found it impossible to reach the holes in her side by heeling the ship. She therefore entered Portsmouth harbour on 28 May with both pumps working. The dockyard carpenters were able to stop her leaks next day, but left several shot embedded in her timbers. The *Britannia*'s bowsprit and foremast were found unserviceable by a surveyor on 5 June. Next day she had a hulk alongside her to heave out the bowsprit and unrig the foremast. The crew got down the main yard and sent that ashore as well. By evening on 7 June she had her new bowsprit, masts and yards in place.

Sails, anchors, cables, all needed survey throughout the fleet, and much required repair or replacement. The ships' carpenters were also busy on the hulls and superstructures and boats. Sir Richard Haddock, Comptroller on the Navy Board, was himself at Portsmouth, busy paying some of the ships' companies and getting the damaged ships ready for sea again. Besides all the repair work, water and provisions had to be embarked, while the Ordnance authorities replenished powder and shot, and replaced damaged guns. In addition there was a requirement for further fireships to replace the nine expended in action. The Admiralty had two under construction, and asked whether any prizes were suitable for fitting out for this role.

Shovell struck his flag on 28 May, and went ashore to Fareham to recover from his wound. Ashby's squadron had been unable to achieve anything at le Havre. Three frigates, sent on ahead, reported on their return that two or three small craft had run into the harbour on their approach. The *Greyhound* went in close enough to count six sail hauled close up under the citadel. Ashby therefore stood over for the English coast. He made a perfect landfall on the Isle of Wight, but mistook the high ground for Beachy Head and bore away down Channel, letting out reefs, until Portland Bill was sighted. Thus it was 29 May before his squadron reached the fleet anchorage. Russell had already instituted patrols off the Start, off Portland and off the Isle of Wight, but it was 4 June before any allied ships were sent back to the coast of France.

There were other things to be done. Two new fighting instructions were added in the light of recent experience: one directed that no disabled ship might leave the line until a flag officer had been informed: flag officers were given authority to relieve any commanding officer who failed in his duty and to appoint another officer in his place. A second new instruction instituted a signal for ordering ships to cut or slip their cables in daylight. All ships were instructed to prepare 'two perfect lists' of men on board at the time of the engagement, so that the bounty money bestowed on them by the queen might be distributed. The money was despatched to Portsmouth on 3 June thanks to a timely loan of £100,000 from the City of London.

It was possibly during this period at the fleet rendezvous, though it may have been before he left the French coast, that Russell wrote to Tourville in order to congratulate him on the extreme valour he had displayed in attacking with so much intrepidity, and in fighting so valiantly although in such unequal strength. He also offered congratulations to the captain of the *Triomphant* in Gabaret's rear squadron, and to d'Amfreville, commanding the van in the *Merveilleux*, though it is a little hard to discern why these two should have been selected for praise by their opponent.

A severe storm starting late on 30 May justified Russell's action in bringing back his damaged fleet to home waters rather than keeping it on the enemy coast for immediate exploitation of his success. Russell landed on that Monday to attend the three privy councillors – Lords Portland, Rochester and Sidney – who had held a council of flag officers on the previous day. He found himself unable to return on board, and was stranded in Portsmouth till the following Friday. Nottingham had respected his request not to publish his report, but had asked for a complete narrative for publication. Russell wrote it from memory whilst ashore, and sent it on its way.

A new 3rd-rate of 80 guns, ready for launching at Portsmouth on 3 June, was named the *Russell*, but the admiral had already personally refused a 'public mark of honour' for his victory. He was, he told Nottingham, past follies of that kind. 'I have no ambition but being thought an honest man, and one that loves my country, for whose liberty I early ventured my all.' He showed something of the same indifference to honours for his subordinates. When asked by the Admiralty to report what commanders and others 'had signalized themselves in the late action', he had no names to put forward. On the other hand he lost no time in bringing to trial two first lieutenants for neglect of their duty in action. Both were dismissed; one, who had remained hidden in the hold during the engagement, was first rowed from ship to ship with a halter round his neck. Russell himself undertook to serve for the rest of the present campaign, but then he would try a little hunting. At least it would not keep him out all night in the wind and rain. He regarded the fact that the fleet was in harbour as not the least part of the good fortune that had attended him; ships still at sea with wounded masts would have run great hazards.[12]

The weather continued vile. Evelyn said that the wind and rain in some places stripped the trees of their fruit and leaves as if it had been winter. The fleet rode secure with topmasts and yards down at St Helen's, but it still had much to do if the initial advantage of its signal victory was to be put to maximum profit.

Chapter 8

Sailmaker: The Britannia *flying the royal standard of William III* (The National Maritime Museum, London).

Indecision   *Summer 1692*

It was as obvious to the administration in London as it was to the commander-in-chief that the victory must be exploited. Russell had much earlier written: 'If we beat them we may follow them, not as they did us, but into their harbours and, embarking soldiers, go for Brest and do a lasting service to England.'[1] With the French fleet scattered, and no doubt demoralized by its heavy losses, he told Nottingham on 25 May, the day after the final scene at la Hougue, that now was the time 'if you were able' to make the descent. Two days later he put it more strongly: 'Now is the time to push it, while the iron is hot, and I am certain France is in a greater fright about the descent than we were here.'[2] Nottingham needed no urging. On the same day, learning that the fleet was in sight from the Isle of Wight, the queen ordered Lords Rochester, Portland and Sidney to Portsmouth to hold a council. She had resolved, Nottingham told Russell, that 'no time shall be lost to prosecute the descent'.[3]

These were fine words, but what had happened to the troops and transports that the king had ordered to be ready by the end of May or early June, just this moment in time? In March Nottingham had listed for Blathwayt, who was with the king in the Netherlands, the forces likely to be available: five regiments of foot (4,000 men) at Portsmouth, and another five (3,500 men) at Cork or Kinsale; ten further regiments of Dutch foot to come from Holland, two regiments of horse and one of dragoons (1,500 men) also at Portsmouth. He had directed the Commissioners of Transport to provide shipping for 3,500 men and 380 horses at Kinsale by the end of March, and for 4,000 men and 1,500 horses in the Thames by the end of April. Victuals for three months would be required, but he had ordered victuals for six months for the indigenous troops so as to conceal the fact that their numbers would be doubled by the addition of the Dutch contingent.

The Transport Commissioners thought that they had shipping immediately available for the troops in the Thames: transports had been provided to take 4,500 Danish troops from Ireland to Ostend, and these were ordered back to the Downs. They arrived there on 3 April, and most of their seamen were immediately pressed to man the fleet, leaving them helpless at anchor and unable to move. A few days later the Admiralty issued a general order that ships were not to press men from transport vessels, and that any men already pressed were to be discharged, but the damage had been done.

On 23 May, one day before the final attack at la Hougue, two troop movements were completed: 52 transports, with five regiments embarked, reached Bristol from Ireland; and three regiments of foot from Scotland, destined for Flanders under Tollemache, reached the Thames.

Tollemache had earlier been released from William's forces in the Low Countries to return to England with three regiments when the threat of invasion was at its height. Except for Marlborough he was probably the best English soldier in William's employ. As colonel of one of the English regiments paid by the States-General, he had brought his men to England in the army of invasion. He had then succeeded Berwick as Governor of Portsmouth, and had fought under Marlborough in the Netherlands in 1689 and as a major-general in Ireland in 1691.

Nottingham directed the three Scots regiments to land at Gravesend, and sent the shipping to the Nore for convoy to Holland to fetch the promised Dutch troops. The artillery train was reported ready in Ireland, with 30 transports to carry to Portsmouth its 30 mortars, 40 cannons, 18 field pieces, 9,000 bombs and 7,000 carcasses (or fire-balls).[4] It looked as if all might quite soon be ready, and on 14 June Carmarthen urged the king to despatch the troops from Holland, and to send a general officer to assist Leinster, who had not the capacity to command infantry.

William, however, had different notions about the further prosecution of the war. The French had laid siege to Namur in mid-May; William, hoping to relieve the rock-fortress, wanted to keep the Dutch troops promised earlier. Nottingham wrote very frankly to Portland pointing out that this decision would be 'of fatal consequence' to Their Majesties' affairs and government. Before the defeat of the French fleet, people had been expecting a descent during the current season; now they would expect it all the more. There were 24 battalions of foot in England; eight were in garrisons, leaving 16 for the descent, a total of 10,000 men. If the king would spare a further 12 battalions (7,800 men) out of the 70,000 in his army, there would be around 18,000 men for the descent.

It was not only troops that William wanted re-disposed; he wanted a naval squadron to be despatched to the Mediterranean. As the head of the alliance ranged against Louis, he wished to give some support to Victor Amadeus of Savoy, one of its weakest members, and to encourage the Spaniards to greater efforts. The government in England, intent on removing the threat of invasion by destroying more of the enemy fleet by attacks on Brest or St Malo, could see no point in such a detachment. Before replying to Blathwayt, who had put forward William's proposal, Nottingham sought Russell's opinion, remarking as he did so that there was no fleet of English merchant vessels requiring protection in the Mediterranean unless another convoy were to be run to the Levant.

Russell replied with a long letter, self-deprecatingly suggesting that it might be a very silly one. It was not: it was an expression of sound strategic thinking, and was woefully prophetic of the mistakes of the next year. Could anyone propose, he asked, that we should be so strong both here and in the Straits, that we might face the French in either? We would not know where the French fleet would be deployed when it was ready for sea. If they chose the Mediterranean, it might be too late, when the news reached England, to prevent a blow more fatal to us than we had just given them. 'Let us take warning from their misfortune,' he concluded, 'not to divide our strength.'[5] Nottingham did not repeat these arguments to Blathwayt for the king's information; he contented himself with saying that all the committee were against sending a squadron to the Mediterranean, and that Admiral Russell was absolutely against it.

These considerations had not yet been deployed when the government representatives and the flag officers met on board the *Britannia* soon after she arrived at St Helen's. The council's resolutions of 30 May were two in number: the first related to the Channel operations, and the second to the despatch of four or five ships to Newfoundland with instructions to do what damage they could to the French there, and to return after about a fortnight. Without waiting for the land forces, Russell was to sail for Ushant with a fleet of not less than 60 ships of the line, sending frigates to determine how many enemy ships were lying in Brest water. It was left to the judgment of flag officers to decide what action to take 'to annoy the enemy', and Russell was to report 'what posture he finds the enemy in'. After 15 days he was to bring the fleet to Torbay for water, and he undertook to keep the ships provisioned for six weeks at sea, provided that this did not extend beyond the end of August.[6] Since it would necessarily be a few days before repair of the fleet flagship and other damaged ships would allow Russell to carry out this plan, the queen was asked to direct him to send a smaller squadron to cruise off Cap de la Hague for two or three days.

The council's resolutions were converted next day into orders from the queen addressed to Russell. He was to send immediately four or five ships, with a fireship if he thought it advisable, under a prudent and experienced officer to endeavour to ruin the French fishery, trade and navigation off Newfoundland. The squadron was to sail with sealed orders, to be opened after passing Land's End, and was to return home after not more than 20 days at its destination. Secondly, he was to send such English and Dutch ships as were ready to cruise for two or three days off Cap de la Hague 'to watch all opportunities of annoying the enemy'.

It was a very small squadron that Russell sent across the Channel in compliance with these orders. It consisted of two 50-gun ships, the *Chester* and *Chatham*, with a Dutch frigate, an English frigate of 16 guns and a fireship. The *Chatham* had taken no part in the actions at Barfleur and la Hougue. Ordered from Falmouth to join the fleet, she had chased off Ushant on 30 May two ships judged to be three-deckers, but they got within the islands. These two can only have been the flagships of Gabaret and Langeron, severely damaged in action, limping in 11 days later. With a little more resolution these two, and their two smaller consorts, might have been taken whilst in the Channel and in sight of the English shore, or intercepted by a superior force off Ushant. The *Chatham* gave up and headed for the Needles channel to rejoin the fleet. The little squadron sailed on the 4th when the weather eased, and was back on the 11th with a few prisoners taken from fishing boats or from a village ashore, including 'a dam'd old ugly woman'. Some houses had been set on fire, much as Tourville's men had fired Teignmouth two summers earlier. Russell, recognizing the similarity, must have hoped to be able to achieve something more worth while.

He had sent two small vessels, one English and one Dutch, over to Guernsey on 7 June to seek news of the French squadron that had escaped; by the 12th, when he went by barge from Spithead to St Helen's to hold a council of flag officers on board the *Neptune*, he had firm intelligence that Pannetier with 25 sail all told, including fireships, was at St Malo. Their damage was repaired, and they were awaiting a chance to reach Brest. So, at least, said the master of a captured French snow. The council recommended that the fleet should sail for a position to intercept the French if they attempted to reach Brest. It recognized that the position could not be held in westerly winds, when the rendezvous was to be Torbay.

Russell sailed on the first day of fair weather, leaving Shovell, who had rehoisted his flag on board the *Duke* at Spithead, to follow with five more ships when they were ready. The commander-in-chief intended to keep west of St Malo, but he soon found that the French coast was a 'very uncertain place for a fleet'. He was still convinced that 'something ought to be hazarded' at St Malo, 'for if those also be destroyed, 'twill put England pretty well at ease for some time'.[7] He had sent Mees in the *Ruby*, with an Anglo-Dutch squadron of nine 54 and 50-gun ships and the *Charles* galley, to cruise between Cap Barfleur and le Havre, and to put ashore all the French prisoners on their own coast. Later Mees was instructed to make a feint attack on la Hougue so as to keep the whole coast in a state of alarm, and to divert attention from St Malo. On 17 June Russell sent another small squadron under Munden of the *Lennox* to cruise off the Seven Islands, west of St Malo, to gain intelligence. They succeeded in burning a French royal fly-boat of 400 tons laden with salt, wine and brandy, all of which had become scarce at ports to the eastward on account of the interruption of coastal trade.

By the end of the month Russell was becoming very anxious for the safety of his large fleet, particularly its great ships, keeping the sea in what had proved appalling Channel weather of winds, fogs and rain, without a single fair day. On the 24th there had been a north-north-westerly gale, which had driven the fleet 60 miles west of Ushant with the usual damage aloft, the *Cornwall* losing her main and mizzen topmasts, while a Dutch ship lost her foremast and bowsprit, and the *Deptford* sprung her mainmast. This storm confirmed him in his view that a fleet ought to be able to drive before a gale for 48 hours in safety if it could not be anchored to ride it out. In the Channel, however, 'six hours with a change of wind makes either side a lee shore'. Conditions were very different from those of the Dutch wars, when the fleets could always anchor in the shoal waters of the North Sea. Just as he had earlier recommended that the fleet ought to be hazarded when there was a prospect of doing some service, so now he equally vehemently protested that its preservation was of so vast a consequence to the nation's welfare that it ought not to be risked without cause.[8] He now intended to take the fleet towards St Malo. If he found it impossible to accomplish anything there, he would return to Torbay, for there was no safe anchorage anywhere on the French coast.

What, meanwhile, had happened to the land forces? Already the king was expressing his concern that the expedition against France had been so long delayed. Portland, after a long and exasperating delay at Harwich, reached the king's camp in the middle of June, and immediately took a hand in the correspondence with Nottingham, explaining why William wanted cavalry sent to him. Nottingham was to send five named regiments of horse to the Netherlands immediately; the transports that had been sent there for infantry had been sent back empty, as none could be spared. Portland emphasized that only infantry were needed for the descent; they could take passage on board warships, and could ruin and burn Rochefort – the whole council at Portsmouth had thought that a feasible operation.

This mention of Rochefort at this stage is the key to the failure of the whole project: there was a distressing lack of higher strategic direction. Though Russell and Nottingham both believed that their object was still the destruction of the French fleet, or a large part of it, in its harbours, here was one of the Privy Council suggesting an attack on Rochefort, to ruin and burn the place.

A month later Carmarthen, still Their Majesties' first minister, had another idea, of which he told the queen, and received her permission to mention it to the king's advisers in the Netherlands, though he kept it secret from the rest of the Cabinet. He pointed out that Louis had ordered the fortification of St Malo and Brest while the expedition was still getting ready to sail; Rochefort was too remote so late in the season. Why not, he argued, attack Dunkirk?

William, at least in the early stages, was fairly consistent, but he was too remote. His interventions served only to confuse his ministers in London. On 20 June he required the attack to be made as soon as possible. He considered the regiments of foot in England sufficient to give a 'helping hand to the burning of French ships at St Malo or Brest, or bombarding those places'. For if, as he had been led to believe earlier in the year, St Malo could be ruined by bombardment without landing a man, how much easier must it be with the support of 16 battalions? At Brest, 2,000 men would be sufficient to take the fort, while the fleet entered Brest water to destroy the enemy warships.[9] He had no general to send to command the infantry under Leinster other than Tollemache, whom he refused to treat as a shuttlecock by sending him back again. He nominated Sir Henry Bellasis for the job.

Nottingham was considerably put out by the order to despatch the five cavalry regiments urgently. He recalled to the Thames sufficient shipping for two regiments just as the transports were dropping down river to go to Portsmouth. The horse were directed to embark at Deptford, and did so on 29 June. This movement, Nottingham told Blathwayt, would mean that there would be insufficient shipping to embark all the foot at Portsmouth. If the other three cavalry regiments were to follow, some regiments of foot would have to be held back for internal security duties.

Thus the whole month of June slipped away. The transports at Bristol refused to sail without an escort stronger than the little frigate *Dolphin* allocated by the Admiralty. They moved across the Bristol Channel to Milford to await sufficient force to deal with the French and Irish privateers they feared. The Admiralty sent the *Richmond* from Chester and further escorts from Falmouth, while Russell detached the *Dragon*. By the end of the month the transports were at long last at Spithead, the artillery transports arrived there on 9 July, and next day the shipping in the Thames, with 40 shallops specially built for landing operations, with skirts fore and aft to keep the men and powder dry, left the Downs for Portsmouth, arriving there with insignificant damage on the 18th.

The foot started embarking four days later, and were all aboard by the 23rd. Two regiments 'a little mutinied' on embarkation, as Nottingham wrote to Southwell, 'for want of their monthly pay'.[10] They were appeased by Bellasis, who told them that he would write for it. Three other regiments lacked their pay, but went on board without incident. The horse, delayed by adverse weather, were embarked on the 25th, and on that evening Leinster went on board the *Breda*, one of the new 3rd-rates just coming into service. Built at Woolwich, her first task had been to escort the transports from the Downs. These new ships formed part of the building programme approved by Parliament at the end of 1690: the *Russell* at Portsmouth has already been mentioned; the *Cornwall*

at Southampton, the *Devonshire* at Bursledon, were two others completed for sea at about this time.

The Admiralty, at Nottingham's request, had asked the Navy Board to
instruct Benbow, after superintending the despatch of the invasion
flotilla from the Thames to the Nore, to attend the Duke of Leinster for
the expedition. Both Leinster and Galway had said that the number of
troops was sufficient, but up to the last moment both complained to the
contrary, and pressed for more horse than could be spared or trans-
ported. Leinster was particularly insistent on the inclusion of dragoons.
No decision had yet been made about the destination of this substantial
expeditionary force. It is therefore difficult to see how any general could
say what cavalry would be required. The truth is that neither Leinster
nor Galway cared for any undertaking of war in which there was no role
for mounted troops. Now that the military force was at last embarked,
the transports must effect a junction with the fleet, so that, in default of
clear instructions from the queen and her council in Whitehall, a decision
on the object of the expedition could at last be taken.

The fleet had not meanwhile been idle, but Russell's visit to the
Channel Islands had brought no useful result and no sign of resolution to
risk an assault. Mees had supplied useful intelligence during a moder-
ately successful cruise. On 19 June off St Malo, he observed 15 ships
lying in a single line in the river, their topmasts struck and no flags or
pendants flying. He approached close enough to have a single gun fired
at him from the shore, but the shot fell short. He reported that the five or
six outermost ships might be destroyed by fireships, supported by
sufficient boats to resist any boats the French might deploy in defence. It
would be necessary to hold one bank of the river with land forces in order
to carry the fire to the innermost ships. It was, he added, no place for
warships. In a later report he quoted one of the local pilots to the effect
that the enemy ships could still remain afloat if moved eight miles up
river, but no notice seems to have been taken of this intelligence, then or
later.

Nine days after his reconnaissance of St Malo, Mees was off Cap
Barfleur, where he landed 100 men. They burned a couple of houses and
brought off some sheep and hogs, and a single prisoner, a corporal of the
militia. This man said that, of the 50,000 men originally encamped at la
Hougue, 18,000 had been re-deployed to protect St Malo and Brest, and
the coasts of Normandy and Britanny. The invasion of England had been
abandoned, and the transports dispersed. Most of the cannon from the
ships destroyed at la Hougue had been salvaged, though some had
melted in the heat of the flames and were unusable. Mees also chased
some enemy small craft into la Hougue, and put some shot among the
boats assisting them to warp into the harbour. Finally, off Cap de la
Hague on 30 June, he fell in with a convoy of 30 ships escorted by three

Danish men-of-war bound for France. He insisted on a search, and brought in three ships carrying contraband in the shape of naval stores.

Mees had one further gain from his efforts – a golden opinion of him from his commander-in-chief. Russell said of him that he did not know 'in all the Navy a more hopeful man', and prophesied that if his life were spared he would make a great man. It was not to be: he was to die at sea as commodore in the West Indies five years later.

Russell anchored the fleet off Guernsey on 3 July in thick weather. No pilot would venture over to St Malo, and Russell complained that the summer had 'produced weather fitting only for Laplanders to be at sea with'.[11] He was not encouraging about the prospect of attacking St Malo with a land force of 12,000 men. He believed that the French had double that number. He suggested to Nottingham that the best use of the expedition would be a landing at la Hougue to bring off the cannon so carefully retrieved by the French from their wrecked warships. This was not one of Russell's most sensible ideas, observing that, for all he knew, the Franco-Irish army might still be 12,000 strong at King James's former camp.

At a council of war on 4 July it was decided that the fleet ought not to run the hazard of anchoring off St Malo. A smaller force should be sent to see if it could ride there, and to reconnoitre anchorages along the coast to the westward. The rest of the fleet was to cruise 24 miles south of the Start; the *Montagu* was sent to Portsmouth to escort the victuallers to the new rendezvous. Rooke, transferred to the *Berwick*, was selected for command of the advanced squadron.

He anchored his Anglo-Dutch squadron off Cap Fréhel on the 5th, and next day sent boats to sound in the bay to the eastward. On the 7th the boats intercepted a French vessel bound for St Malo with salt; her crew escaped ashore, whence a chance shot killed the captain of the fireship *Griffin*. On 9 July the squadron moved further east, but two days later, when it was near Jersey, the wind began to blow hard from the north-west. Unable to weather the Caskets, Rooke bore away through the Alderney race as Carter had done in May, and on 13 July rejoined Russell in Torbay.

The commander-in-chief had been driven to the anchorage four days earlier, leaving the *Deptford* to cruise at the rendezvous. A month had already gone by since the fleet had repaired its action damage. Russell pointed out that though there had so far been no fine weather, the summer would be over in another six weeks. And every day of delay made the task of assault more difficult; already there was a requirement for twice as many troops as would have sufficed a month earlier.

Rooke's report was not encouraging. There were some sandy bays east of Cap Fréhel, but they were dominated by rising ground, and any force landed there would have to cross a river to reach St Malo. The tides ran very fast along the shore, as well they might, for there is a rise and fall of 40 feet at the harbour. There were still over 30 enemy ships there, but none of the pilots would take a warship or fireship into St Malo, though Rooke had 'offered £100 encouragement to each man'.[12] A council of war, called by Rooke on board the *Berwick* on 8 July and attended by Callenburg, ten captains and 12 pilots, had concluded that the fleet could not come to St Malo without great hazard, nor could it lie off Cap Fréhel. A squadron might be ventured off the town in order to cover the landing of troops from transports, provided that the fleet was disposed so as to prevent any enemy interference from the westward.

A further council of war at Torbay decided to maintain a squadron in a position to intercept and report any attempt by the St Malo ships to reach Brest. Russell detailed Neville in the *Kent* for this duty, with 13 English and eight Dutch ships of the line, four Dutch frigates, and five fireships from the two fleets. They parted company on 17 July off the Start. For the next two days the main fleet was enshrouded in thick fog; Russell took advantage of the first clear patch to run back to Torbay to victual his ships.

The queen's orders had now been issued, and were typical of a document emanating from a committee. Leinster was told to embark 17 regiments of foot and 200 dragoons, and to proceed with all expedition to the fleet, 'where he shall concert with the flag and field officers what may be attempted upon the enemy'. The queen did not think it proper to enjoin any particular enterprise, yet she particularly recommended to him the destruction of St Malo and Brest, of the magazines at Brest and Rochefort, and of the transport ships at la Hougue and le Havre. Leinster was required to propose all these things at a council of war, and to execute them 'in such manner and order as shall be thought most proper'. The political aim, of removing the invasion threat for the rest of the war by completing the destruction of the French fleet, had disappeared in a welter of choices of schemes designed only to annoy the enemy.

The orders to Russell were a bit firmer. He was instructed to act with the fleet to assist the troops under the Duke of Leinster as judged proper at a council of war, 'in the first place as to taking or burning the town of St Malo and the shipping there', and then the pursuit of those of the other recommended objectives as might be judged feasible.

The troop convoy cleared the Isle of Wight with a north-east wind on 27 July, whilst in London wagers were being laid on its objective, and met the fleet next morning. Fortunately the weather was fair; after the duke and the admiral had dined together a very large council of war sat for three hours on board the *Breda*. All the flag officers, English and Dutch, were present, as were Leinster and eight military officers, including Galway and Bellasis. The council heard the evidence of Rooke and

Callenburg about the approaches to St Malo. They concluded that the fleet could do nothing against the enemy ships there till the town had been so far reduced by the action of the land forces that ships might approach without much annoyance from enemy guns. But the army representatives said that they could do nothing there without the assistance of the fleet.

So the project for a descent on the coast of France, so long planned, so painfully prepared, evaporated in this sterile discussion on board the new 3rd-rate *Breda*, lifting to the Channel swell south of the Start. For the flag officers considered the season too far advanced to attempt anything against Brest or Rochefort. They thought that the fleet could lie in safety between la Hougue and le Havre, and could protect the army ashore in those parts until the end of August. Leinster evidently thought that they were sailing off to 'annoy the enemy' on the coast of Normandy, but the fleet, less a sizeable detachment sent to relieve Neville on patrol, lingered uncertainly off the English coast, and Russell sat down next day, as the *Britannia* lay off Portland, to pour out his thoughts to Nottingham without the least reserve.

He started by emphasizing the hazards of operations off St Malo, where the tides ran swiftly and there were many rocks which could not be avoided if the enemy moved the navigation marks, or vision were to be obscured by smoke. As the queen had persisted in recommending action there, he had thought that she must have some information that the land forces could do something against the town. But Her Majesty's order of 14 July had left the choice of objective to a council of war. It was the first time he had ever heard of numbers of men being embarked and sent to sea before a resolution had been taken where they should go, and whether or not they could achieve anything. It had been fortunate that the transports had not been driven out of the Channel by a strong easterly wind.

Next he set about demolishing the proposed operations one by one. St Malo: if it appeared in June to be hardly practicable at any time, it must be more difficult in August weather, when the enemy had been given two months to prepare a defence. Brest: an attack might have been possible in June or early July, but if the wind were to stay in the west for two or even three months at a stretch, what would become of the fleet and army? Rochefort: this had been mentioned at the council at Portsmouth at the end of May, when it was expected that the troops would be ready in 20 days; but the design had soon afterwards been laid aside because the place was too far for the fleet to go; it was still too far, and more hazardous at the later season.

The destruction of one of these three objectives would have been of some use to England, for it was there that the enemy's naval forces lay. If the queen thought one of them attackable, positive orders ought to have been sent. 'Then we had nothing to consider but the well performance of those orders.' Now the council had determined to attack la Hougue. Forgetting his own recommendation made so shortly before, Russell said that this would be no more a service than an accidental fire in Knightsbridge would be a disservice. His mind was obviously turning back again to the futility of Teignmouth, and he was hurt that he had been unable to achieve more as a result of his victory than had Tourville.

In the period that elapsed between the issue of the orders from Whitehall on 14 July and the departure of the transports on the 27th, a report had come in of a squadron of warships off Ushant. In London this was supposed to refer to the enemy ships from St Malo, though Russell at once perceived that it probably related to Neville's squadron. Some time later, when Neville returned to harbour, Russell was proved right. Neville remembered one of his ships, the *Monk*, chasing the vessel whose captain had made the report, and said that six Ostenders bound for Corunna with troops had added to the amount of shipping in the neighbourhood at the time. The false deduction at Whitehall caused the queen to send revised instructions to the fleet. Russell was told, in an order dated 26 July, to 'consider what may be attempted upon Brest, or for the destruction of the ships in that bay or harbour'. He was to reconnoitre St Malo, and put into execution any resolution relating to Brest before considering at a council of war which other enterprise ought to be pursued. The burning of St Malo was again particularly recommended.

The receipt of these revised instructions caused another council of war to be summoned on board the *Breda* off St Alban's Head on 30 July. The assembled admirals and generals saw no reason to alter the opinions that they had expressed in the resolutions passed at their previous meeting. But as the queen had laid such stress on the destruction of St Malo, they resolved to take the fleet and transports to St Helen's so that they might be kept together, and there to await orders, 'which, if contrary to the opinions of the council of war, we desire may be positive'. Russell was dreadfully upset at the mortification of finding that nothing could be done. He was out of touch with Ashby, who had been detached to relieve Neville; but Neville had not yet rejoined him. He asked Nottingham, if he really believed that the St Malo ships had reached Brest, to recall Ashby by sending orders to Dartmouth, to which port Ashby had been told to send in frequently.

The result of the first council of war had been received with consternation in Whitehall; Nottingham's confidence in Russell was beginning to crack. Very little could be expected, he told Portland, from a man out of humour. He believed, he wrote to Blathwayt, that the king would be extremely surprised at the decisions reached by his land and sea officers. He did not want William to think that the conduct of affairs by the queen in council had been so absurd and ridiculous as Russell had represented it. Mary herself had earlier found Russell's letters strangely worded, with his constant appearance of dissatisfaction and his talk of retiring. He seemed to her to be hindering as much as he could; at least he forwarded nothing.

In a difficult position, the queen issued new orders, this time specifying an attack on St Malo. Though Russell would remain in command of the fleet, he was to detail a vice admiral or rear admiral to take all the English and Dutch ships of the 3rd rate and below, and to escort the transports and shallops as near to St Malo as possible. The frigates and fireships were to go into the roads, but the rest of the squadron was to lie to the westward, as recommended by Rooke's council of war, so as to protect the assault from enemy interference. Russell was to take the allied 1st and 2nd rates to Torbay, and to be ready to go to the assistance of the detached squadron if the French fleet from Brest were to intervene. Orders were despatched to Ashby to take his great ships to Torbay, and to send the rest to join the St Malo squadron. The queen's order to Leinster was short and sharp. He was told in a couple of lines to go to St Malo, and to burn the town and the ships.

At last the government was telling its fighting men what it wanted done, and indicating sufficiently the manner in which its orders were to be carried out. It was a thousand pities that it had not done so sooner. It was left to the commander-in-chief to select the naval commander for the expedition – Nottingham expected Delaval, Rooke or Shovell to be chosen – but he was not to have a hand in the execution of the attack. In the two months since the battles of Barfleur and the Hogue he had utterly forfeited the trust of the administration.

No sooner had these new orders been despatched than Nottingham received the further shock of the result of the second council of war. Mary found Russell's letter announcing the fleet's return to St Helen's, on top of the stillborn project against la Hougue, 'which was worse than nothing', a real trouble and vexation. There was nothing for the council to do but to go to the fleet and argue the matter with the admirals and generals. With Carmarthen the Lord President at their head, five members of the queen's council were to go, accompanied by the First Lord of the Admiralty and the Secretary of State. They would reach Portsmouth on the night of 2 August; Nottingham asked Russell to send his yacht to bring them all aboard on the following morning.

Then came the surprise, the unexpected intervention of the king. It allowed both the executive and the military to put aside their quarrel, and to concentrate on carrying out the new royal wishes.

William had tried to attack the French army with his right wing. Initially successful, his troops had been driven back by a counter-attack, and both sides had suffered very heavy casualties, amounting to

7,000 men each. This setback, known as the battle of Steinkirk, caused him to search for some other means of achieving a military success in the Low Countries before the end of the year's campaign. To bombard Dunkirk, and to render it useless to the enemy, seemed a very worthwhile project. The seed sown by Carmarthen had grown into a strong shoot. If the admirals and generals should decide not to attack St Malo or Brest, and in that event only, William wanted all transports sent to the Downs to await orders. He seemed assured that things would have turned out in this fashion, for he sent his Adjutant-General of Foot to convey his intentions to Nottingham, and then to the fleet.

The king's new initiative, conveyed in a letter from Blathwayt to Nottingham and brought by the Adjutant-General, reached the Secretary of State at Portsmouth in time to prevent acrimony at the meeting between the lords of the council and the senior naval and military officers. Nottingham said in reply that the king's orders would be carried out sooner than he could have expected. Leinster was ordered to land the dragoons and two regiments to garrison Portsmouth, and to remain on board with the rest. To meet his objection that the troops were too crowded, Russell arranged for some of them to be transferred to the hospital ships, which had happily not been required for their proper duties.

The lords were back at Whitehall by the evening of the 4th, and next day the queen again despatched new orders to the fleet. Russell was to detach an allied squadron of eight warships and six fireships under a flag officer; it was to convoy the transports, the shallops and a bomb vessel to the Downs or to Margate road. Another naval requirement had arisen: information had been received that allied shipping might be stopped by the Danes in the Sound, and that naval stores on board might be seized. Russell was therefore directed to send another squadron, consisting of at least ten ships, under 'a prudent and fit' officer, to protect allied interests in the approaches to the Baltic. He was given discretion to await the return of Ashby's squadron from the French coast before he complied.

Shovell was detailed for the convoy to the Downs, and arrived there in the *Kent* on the evening of 8 August. And there, unfortunately, transports and escorts remained for over ten days awaiting orders. Leinster was becoming restive, as sickness began to show itself among the troops, and asked for instructions to be given for the marine hospital at Deal to receive the infectious cases; about 60 men were later put ashore. Shovell's orders, when they came, told him to be at Ostend or Nieuport on 22 or 23 August, or a day or two earlier if the weather were fine; the artillery was to be landed there, and the rest of the troops as near as possible to Ostend. He was warned that only ships with a draught of eight feet or less could enter Nieuport. There was a misunderstanding about the shipment of hay for the artillery and other horses still embarked; when this had been satisfactorily settled, the convoy sailed at last for the coast of Flanders, arriving off Ostend on 21 August in the evening.

The Dutch commodore had assembled over 30 local pilots to take the larger transports into harbour, followed by the smaller vessels, and protected by the *Charles* galley and three small Dutch frigates. The *Mary* yacht, which William had used to land at Carrickfergus, carried Leinster ashore, but he was not to have a success comparable to the Boyne. William detached troops under Tollemache from his main army, and sent cannon down the Meuse from Maastricht, but to no avail. The shallops proved a failure as supports for the troops along the coast. They could not endure any kind of bad weather, and most of them were sent back to Chatham early in September. Of the four that were kept, two were later wrecked and the other two driven across the straits to the English coast.

Dunkirk was found to be too strong, and William had to be content with the capture of Dixmude and Furne, and their fortification to improve the frontier defences for the winter. It was a small enough result for all the effort that had gone into the planned descent of 1692. The cannon were sent back up the Meuse, and the troops came home in the middle of October. William himself had a disturbing experience on 8 September, when the house in which he was dining was violently shaken by an earthquake lasting a minute. A late move by the French against Charleroi caused him to delay his departure for England, and the queen became anxious about his safety. But on 18 October, after a rough passage, he landed at Yarmouth, and took coach for London. Tourville alleges that, sighting four enemy vessels on the way over, William had his standard taken in lest its display should encourage them to attack. After a night at Colchester, where Mary met the king, Their Majesties were received with acclamation in the City as they made their way back to Kensington.

Russell had left the fleet early in September, directing that the *Fubbs* yacht should bring his effects to Greenwich as soon as the fleet flagship could spare her. Already there were rumours that he would be removed from his command, but he went off to the Earl of Bedford's seat at Woburn to enjoy some leisure after what had proved a trying period of four months afloat. The last month at St Helen's, after Shovell had sailed with the transports, had been fully occupied in disposing the fleet to meet the many commitments that remained. He detailed Robinson of the *Monmouth* for command of the squadron for the Sound, though as a 'blundering fellow' it is doubtful whether he would have been successful in any mission requiring a display of diplomacy. Fortunately the Danish attitude softened, Robinson's ships were held in the Downs, and before the end of August 45 ships left the Baltic without hindrance, carrying much-needed naval stores. Ashby's squadron, which had relieved Neville watching for any movement of the St Malo ships, rejoined the fleet in mid-August.

The weather of that dreadful summer remained as bad as ever. In a violent thunderstorm the *Adventure* was struck by lightning, her mainmast was shattered, and two men were killed. Two fireships also suffered damage. The dirty weather allowed Russell to feel vindicated; his argument that the season was too far advanced for operations had been backed by a demonstration by the forces of nature. Although he had received a direct order from the queen to take the fleet to Torbay, he never succeeded in leaving the Isle of Wight anchorage, pleading in extenuation that all the flag officers believed that 'in point of seamanship' the fleet should remain where it was.

Once Ashby's squadron had been removed from its intercepting station without replacement, Forbin, still commanding the *Perle*, came out of St Malo with two other ships of comparable size. Off the Lizard, at the end of August, they approached a Dutch convoy of 70 ships, escorted by two men-of-war. The Dutch mistook them for English ships, particularly as they showed English colours until close enough to attack. Both the Dutch escorts were taken, but the merchant vessels escaped. In anticipation of their arrival in south-western ports, Russell had sent four ships to Plymouth for onward escort duties. The Dutch had maintained a squadron under Count van Nassau at sea for nearly a month awaiting the convoy, which had somehow eluded friend and met foe.

Forbin's little force was not the only threat: it seems that Nesmond came out cruising from Brest; and all the time the privateers exerted their pressure.

Finally, on 14 September, intelligence reached the fleet, from a French storeship captured off Portland on the 10th, that the rest of the French had left St Malo on the 7th, and had anchored for a couple of days off Cap Fréhel with no wind before getting an easterly to carry them towards Brest. The *London Gazette* reported on 17 September that four days earlier a Dutch privateer off the Isle de Basse had fallen in with 22 French sail bound from St Malo to Brest. There were 16 men-of-war and six flyboats, one of which the Dutchman managed to capture. Ashby, who had taken command of the winter squadron, sailed on receipt of the news, but of course he was too late to effect an interception.

The squadron returning with five prizes from its raid on the Newfoundland fisheries was dispersed by the weather, turning up in October, one or two at a time at ports along the south coast.

Thus the year's naval operations came to an end. They had started brilliantly with the most complete victory attained against the French until the Seven Years' War over 60 years later. After the battle, almost nothing seemed to have gone right, and the activities of enemy privateers, including five or more carrying James's commission, had brought grievous losses to English and Dutch trade. The army had cost much money and had achieved little. The harvest had failed. When William opened Parliament on 4 November, his 42nd birthday, he was ready for a storm of criticism. Many Tories were opposed to him personally, many Whigs to monarchy itself. It was going to be difficult to raise money to continue the struggle, and many questions were going to be asked about the conduct of the campaign of 1692.

Chapter 9

Louis XIV of France, engraving after H. Rigaud (photo: H. Roger-Viollet).

Retribution 1693

William presented a bold face to his Parliament. His speech congratulated the English on the valour they had displayed by land and sea. It was painful to call upon them for further sacrifices, but no good Englishman and no good Protestant should shrink from those necessary for the safety of the nation and its religion.

Since William's accession revenue had been raised yearly by a tax on the value of land. After a new valuation in 1692 it was estimated that a tax of one shilling in the pound would raise £½ million. To the astonishment of Louis, Parliament fixed it at four shillings for 1693, to raise £2 million, and in December introduced the novel expedient of raising a further million pounds by borrowing. From this modest beginning the national debt came into existence.

Parliament found other things in which to interest itself, notably the failure to follow up the naval success of early summer, and complaints on all sides that commerce had not been better protected. Nottingham had to defend his conduct in the Lords, while Russell was forced to do so in the Commons. Not surprisingly, each house was soon defending its own member against the other, and the two men were set resolutely at loggerheads. It was not only a quarrel between the two houses; it was also a quarrel between the two parties. The Tories blamed the Whig admiral; the Whigs blamed the Tory administrator. Only Carmarthen held aloof and blamed neither. Macaulay's magisterial summing up of the characters of the two men facing each other in this difference of opinion deserves quotation in full.

> Nottingham was a Tory: Russell was a Whig. Nottingham was a speculative seaman, confident of his theories: Russell was a practical seaman, proud of his achievements. The strength of Nottingham lay in speech: the strength of Russell lay in action. Nottingham's demeanour was decorous even to formality: Russell was passionate and rude. Lastly, Nottingham was an honest man; and Russell was a villain. They now became mortal enemies. The Admiral sneered at the Secretary's ignorance of naval affairs; the Secretary accused the Admiral of sacrificing the public interests to mere wayward humour; and both were in the right.[1]

As so often in the affairs of men, things had gone wrong in spite of the best endeavours of those trying to control events. Nottingham defended himself well in the upper house, and laid on the table a mass of papers for their lordships to examine. They did so, and reached conclusions by no means favourable to Russell. They would not, however, condemn him unheard; they sent all the papers to the Commons with a call for Russell to answer the case against him. The Commons had already heard Russell, and paid perfunctory attention to the new material before resolving that the admiral had behaved 'with fidelity, courage and conduct'. They appreciated, from the evidence of the Commissioners for Transport and the Commissioners of Victualling, that a want of sufficient and timely supplies had hindered the public service by contributing to the fatal delays of the summer campaign. They did their best to remedy this, and voted almost £2 million for the Royal Navy and the Ordnance, to cover the completion of a yard at the Hamoaze off Plymouth Sound and the building of four bomb vessels and eight new 4th-rates, in addition to the usual annual charges.

In furtherance of their quarrel with the Lords, the Commons first proposed a resolution asking the king to constitute a Board of Admiralty composed of persons of known experience in maritime affairs, but this was not accepted by the Lords. They next attempted a motion that all orders for the future management of the fleet should pass through the hands of the Admiralty Commissioners. It was an implied criticism of the Secretary of State's handling of the campaign. Ideally the statesman's task is to give a broad directive to the Admiralty, and to allow the Commissioners full discretion to arrange all the details. But Nottingham had issued orders from the queen direct to the commander-in-chief, specifying the numbers and types of ships he was to employ for various purposes. It would not do. The Whigs in the Commons attempted to censure Nottingham, but he found a champion in his fellow-Tory Lowther, who had proved the lynch-pin of the ministry, a genial, solid man who now declared that Their Majesties had no more zealous or faithful servant than the Secretary of State.

The longer the quarrel lasted, the more certain it became that either Nottingham or Russell would have to go. Both the king and the queen were determined to keep Nottingham as their Secretary of State; since Russell refused to serve afloat if Nottingham remained, it followed that he would not command the fleet for 1693. William considered indeed that the admiral had shown a much greater concern for his own interest and reputation than for his service to the monarchy. Notwithstanding the great things he had done, Russell must be laid aside for the present.

When it came to choosing a successor, the curious, and in the event disastrous, idea was revived of sharing the responsibility among three admirals. It was suggested that the charge of so great a fleet was too much for one man, an argument that Russell had himself put forward in 1690. The truth was rather that the custom then prevalent, of calling councils of flag officers whenever an important decision was required, tended to stifle initiative, and to inhibit a bold and active policy. Few committees in history have failed to listen to voices urging caution.

Tourville had stood firm on at least two occasions. As he approached Brest from the Mediterranean in 1689, his juniors advised him to put back so as to avoid the risk of meeting the allied fleet off Ushant. But he knew that, if he held off until there was a good westerly gale, the enemy would be driven off station, and he would be carried into harbour. And thus it turned out. Again, as already described, he ordered the attack at Barfleur in spite of marked inferiority in strength and his subordinates' disinclination to fight against such odds. Russell's decisions, on the other hand, seem always to have commanded the support of his junior flag officers. This is not to say that he was always right, nor that he did all that with hindsight it can be seen was open to him. But there was never any doubt of his capacity to command, nor that he, like Tourville, had the will to over-ride, if necessary, the opinions of others. On at least two occasions he found it convenient to ignore the resolutions of councils of war: after the successes of Cherbourg and la Hougue it was decided that the bulk of the allied fleet should move westward towards Brest, yet Russell, as already related, took the fleet back to England; later, when the joint council of admirals and generals advised making for the east of the Cotentin peninsula, he chose to linger off the English coast till fresh circumstances arose to compel a return to harbour. To suggest that the job was too big for him, or for any one man, was therefore absurd. To vest the command of a great fleet in a permanent committee of three was to invite caution, or indecision, or perhaps defeat.

The appointments were not made till January; Killigrew, Delaval and Shovell were selected. The first two were Tories; Shovell, in so far as he had political convictions of any kind, was a Whig. A Dutch cartoon of the period represented Shovell with his hands tied behind his back, the ends of the cord being held by the other two admirals. Though interpreted in England as bearing a political inference, it may be that the picture was an attempt to show the Dutch assessment of the relative fighting capacities of the three admirals. It was an inauspicious beginning.

Evelyn, who a month earlier had noted that the quarrel between Russell and Nottingham was 'yet undetermined', recorded early in February: 'Our Admiral Russell laid aside for not pursuing the advantage he had against the French the past summer: three others chosen in his place.'[2] Pepys, who was still keeping an eye on naval affairs, commented on the nation's imperfect judgment of anything relating to the sea, citing as an example the irreconcilable differences between the resolutions carried by the Lords and the Commons, the one in favour of

Nottingham, the other of Russell. These opposite resolutions remained on record, with no regard for the truth, and the matter wholly undecided between them.[3]

Russell, though he must naturally have been hurt, was probably not sorry to be spared another long summer afloat. He was offered and accepted an appointment as Treasurer of the Household, and on 28 March kissed hands as Governor of the Isle of Wight. Life at Court suited him better than service afloat, even though he was actively disliked by many men of considerable influence there, and knew it. He was very content to settle down to enjoy the blessings of the land with the fruits of his labours. Unfortunately the size of the fruits did not match his expectations.

Quite aside from the confidence of both king and queen in the energy and abilities of Nottingham as Secretary of State, it is likely that William's disenchantment with Russell stemmed at least partially from the admiral's importunity for money. It appears that in the winter of 1691–2 the king had acceded to a request to make him a gift to the value of seven or eight thousand pounds, and that, shortly before His Majesty's departure for Holland in the spring of 1692, Russell had asked for the grant of some buildings off Suffolk Street, north of Whitehall. In May the title was made over to him, but he found to his chagrin that vacant possession could not be obtained for 27 years, and that he could not therefore obtain any kind of offer for the property. In the following winter he returned to the king, who told him to find something else on which to raise the capital he wanted. He considered the manufacture of farthings, but the Lords of the Treasury were cool to the proposal, and he soon recognized the likely difficulties and delays in proceeding with that idea. By May of 1693 he was sorely in need of cash, for he had embarked on the building of a country mansion, and his own expenses on the transport and entertainment of the Queen of Spain in 1690, and on the three sea campaigns of 1689, 1691 and 1692, made it impossible to finish the work from his own resources.

Faced with this crisis in his affairs, he wrote at length to Lord Portland, setting out the history of his request, pointing out the services he had rendered to the king, from the inception of the invasion project in the summer of 1688 to his leaving the sea in the preceding winter, and finally begging Portland to intercede with the king on his behalf. The idea he now put forward was a royal grant of two-thirds of the proceeds of the sale of timber from the Forest of Dean for four years, producing £2,000 a year, and a total of exactly the sum which the king had agreed to bestow on him. No doubt both the king and his minister had many other matters to occupy their attention as they wrestled with the political and military problems of 1693. Early in July, when Russell again wrote to Portland, this time on behalf of his brother, he had still heard nothing about his own plea.[4] Considering the honours and fortunes heaped on successful naval and military commanders in this and other ages, Russell's rewards had been meagre in the extreme.

While Russell struggled with the provision of finance for establishing himself in the country in the style to which he was accustomed, the business of government and of the fleet went forward as usual. Rooke was promoted to vice admiral of the red, Aylmer to rear admiral of the red; Berkeley was made vice admiral of the blue, and Mitchell left his staff appointment to become rear admiral of the blue. William visited Portsmouth in mid-February, dined on board Rooke's flagship, and knighted him in recognition of his part in the victory at la Hougue. According to a contemporary biographer, it was said that Sir George also received an annuity of £1,000. If true, the income was no doubt a due reward for the destruction of 12 enemy warships, four of them of the largest size. But in that event Delaval, who had destroyed three, and Russell, who had been in overall command of both successes, should in justice have received comparable rewards. The reason for the discrimination, if it occurred, may lie in Rooke's more sympathetic character, in contrast to Russell's querulousness and Delaval's frequent requests for favour.

Delaval had recovered from a heavy fall from his horse when riding to Portsmouth at the end of the previous November, and on 28 April the three admirals exercising the command in chief attended an important meeting in London. Plans for the campaign of 1693 were discussed with ministers and with the army commanders. St Malo and Rochefort were mentioned again, only to be turned down as objectives. It was agreed that a fleet of 65 or more ships should be sailed so as to reach Brest before the French could come out, and before reinforcements from Toulon could reach them. The admirals thought it unlikely, however, that the Dutch would hazard their ships in an attempt to destroy the enemy fleet in the roadstead.

After those attending the meeting had dispersed, Shovell came back for a private word with Carmarthen, who had presided. Just as the Dutch would not make an attack without positive orders, he said, so excuses would be made by the English if discretion should again be left, as in the previous year, to a council of war. Carmarthen heeded this advice, and wrote to the king on the same day recommending the issue of precise instructions to the fleet. It was planned to embark about 5,000 troops in the warships. Their role was to assist on board in the close fighting expected between ships in Brest water, after taking the batteries at the entrance. Five regiments for this purpose were already quartered near Portsmouth.

All these plans ignored two important but conflicting requirements: firstly, William had at last persuaded the Admiralty to send a squadron into the Mediterranean; and secondly, the Levant company had been pressing since the previous June for the despatch of a convoy to Smyrna, and there was a vast amount of other shipping awaiting escort to Spain and Portugal, and across the Atlantic.

Russell had long before given his views on the dangers to be encountered by a convoy bound for the Mediterranean, and more particularly on its return. In the previous July he recommended a policy of deception. If publicity were given to the inclusion of contingents of shipping for Cadiz, Alicante and Leghorn, the French would be led to station ships to lie in wait in the most convenient waters for effecting interceptions. Then the convoy, containing only vessels bound for the Levant, was to keep well to the westward of the coast of Portugal, make a landfall on the African coast, and hug the Barbary shore till it reached Tunis. It was an excellent plan, and it appealed to Nottingham. Unfortunately the merchants desiring convoy to Spanish and Italian ports were just as insistent as those of the Levant company, and there was no escape from treating the whole movement of shipping as one operation.

The month of May had as usual arrived before the allies were ready to act. They suffered a setback when the *Windsor Castle* ran on the Tongue shoal off Margate after leaving the Medway, and became a total loss. Rooke was to command the squadron for the Mediterranean, his flag in the 70-gun *Royal Oak*, with 13 ships of the line, both English and Dutch, and two fireships. After seeing the convoy safely through the straits, he was to join forces with the Spanish fleet, and was to make use of Spanish harbours, Cartagena on the mainland and Port Mahon in Minorca, as advanced bases. Because of the threat from the enemy fleet in Brest, which might at any time be reinforced from Toulon as in previous years, the sailing of the convoy was delayed till the Grand Fleet was ready for sea.

There was a further conference at Portsmouth on 15 May, attended by five Lords of the Council in addition to the allied admirals. All present were satisfied that the Brest fleet was still in port, though it was on that very day completing its movement to the roadstead in readiness to sail. There was, however, no intelligence on the whereabouts of the Toulon squadron. The conference therefore decided that the Smyrna convoy must wait with its escort at St Helen's until some news of this hostile force was received. If it then appeared that the French fleet was concentrated, the Grand Fleet should accompany the convoy 'so far as a council of war should think proper'.

This decision was, however, over-ruled a few days later. In obedience to the queen's commands, the Admiralty directed that the Grand Fleet should sail in company with the Mediterranean squadron, escorting the convoys for Bilbao, Virginia and the Straits, and should detach the Mediterranean portion to steer a safe course for Cadiz. A council of war, summoned on receipt of these orders, decided that a position 90 miles west-south-west of Ushant would be a suitable place to part company. Danby, now commanding the refitted *Royal William*, urged strongly at this time the importance of sending a squadron to reconnoitre Brest, and offered to take a single ship to do the job himself; but it appears that the commanders of this enormous concourse of shipping set sail with no knowledge of the whereabouts of the enemy, and an assumption, already incorrect, that its main fleet was still at Brest.

There was no further news when the position for parting company was reached on 4 June. On that morning a blue flag hoisted at the main topmast head of the *Britannia*, and the firing of three guns, gave the signal to Rooke to proceed in execution of his orders. However the three admirals decided, 'in consideration we have no intelligence where the enemy is',[5] to stay with the convoy for a further 60 miles. Rooke was therefore suprised to see, throughout the 5th and 6th, the sails of the Grand Fleet still in sight to the northward. On the 7th there was no further sign of them; Rooke and his subordinate flag officers shifted their flags to positions appropriate to an independent command. The Grand Fleet, 45 English and 24 Dutch ships of the line, had turned back for its general rendezvous 30 miles north-west of Ushant.

The admirals' decision was based on the false premise that the French fleet was still at Brest, and therefore between the Grand Fleet and its bases in England and Holland. If it were true, the south coast of England lay open to invasion unless the allied fleet returned to protect it, a consideration that weighed heavily with the admirals.

It was not till 17 June that the *Warspite* returned from a reconnaissance to report that Brest was empty except for a few fishing boats. Still thinking of their primary duty of protecting the Kingdom, the admirals stood north for the Scillies, and put in to Torbay on 21 June.

The Admiralty had meanwhile learnt the truth. A report from the consul at Leghorn received on 13 June put the Toulon squadron a short time earlier at Marseilles, ready to sail with 35 galleys. The presence of the galleys suggested that the squadron was to be employed on the Catalan coast, as indeed it was. Soon afterwards two independent reports came in that Tourville with over 100 sail was in the bay of Lagos. Evelyn had already guessed the outcome before the end of May. Recording the sailing of the allied fleet and the French inferiority in strength, "tis believed,' he wrote, 'they will avoid us, and lie in wait for our Turkey merchants, which would be to them a rich prize and to us an irreparable loss, which might have been prevented if leave had been given for their sailing in February.'[6]

While Evelyn's opinion was based on hearsay, the king in the Netherlands had better information, and became seriously alarmed when on 31 May he received a copy of the decision of the council of war that the fleet should leave the convoy when clear of Ushant. He realized that it was based on an assumption, astonishing in the circumstances of the truth being discoverable by a small fast-sailer, that the Toulon squadron had joined Tourville at Brest. William's concern mounted when, almost three weeks later, he heard simultaneously that the main French fleet had been seen off Cadiz, and that the main allied fleet had left the convoy.

The reports of Tourville were true enough: the French had moved first, and were well placed for the interception. Tourville, made a marshal of France in March and a knight of the newly established military order of St Louis in April, was ready to leave Brest by the middle of May. His battle fleet, about 70 strong, with fireships, storeships and despatch vessels in company, sailed out of Berteaume roads on the 16th. The fleet formed up in six columns and stood south-west across the Bay of Biscay, keeping well clear of Cape Finisterre so as to avoid chance sightings and consequent reports of his movements. The flag officers were mainly those who had served the previous year, with a replacement for d'Amfreville, who had died in December at the age of 50. Off the Portuguese coast the fleet was spread in line abreast at wide intervals so that it covered a front of over 70 miles. Tourville had revealed to his senior officers his plan to intercept the allied convoy bound for the Levant, and was encouraged when he obtained news that it would contain vessels bound for Cadiz and Italy as well as for Smyrna. There was mist off Cape St Vincent, so he formed his fleet into three columns, and ran past the cape to anchor off Sagres, showing English and Dutch colours. He intended to ventilate the ships, re-provision them and careen some, while he waited for his prey to fall into the trap. He sent an English-speaking officer ashore, and made use of the services of Henry Fitzjames to welcome on board representatives of the governor and captain-general of the Algarve. But the deception could not long be maintained; the admiral was soon exchanging gifts with the reputedly neutral governor, who showed every sign of amity.

It was not till 16 June, after almost a month of waiting, that reports came in from two scouting frigates that 150 sail in three columns were 45 miles distant from Cape St Vincent. The French fleet stood out to sea at dusk. Tourville did not know for certain that this was the convoy he was expecting. It might be the Grand Fleet itself, and he had no intention of fighting another Barfleur when the enemy held the weather gauge. He therefore deliberately lost ground to leeward during the night so as to be closer to d'Estrées and his squadron, whom he expected from the Mediterranean.

As Rooke passed down the coast of Portugal the consul at Lisbon attempted to send him word of the danger for which he was heading. The fort at the mouth of the Tagus would not let the vessel sail with the warning despatch, the governor maintaining that it would be a breach of neutrality. Nevertheless, as he approached Cape St Vincent, Rooke sent ahead the small frigate *Lark* as a scout. Unfortunately she became becalmed as she approached the shore, and it was not till next day that he obtained his first indication of an enemy presence when two of his ships engaged two French warships and sighted eight or ten more lying under the cape. Rooke called his two flag officers, Hopson and Van der Goes, to a council. While Rooke was in favour of laying by all night, so as to be sure of the size of the opposing force before risking an engagement, the others were for taking advantage of a fresh northerly wind to stand on for Cadiz. Not satisfied, Rooke called in five or six captains to give their opinion: all were for pressing on. The squadron and its charge therefore ran along the shore all night, forcing some French ships still in Lagos bay to cut their cables, and capturing a fireship and some small craft. The captain of the fireship gave the false impression that the enemy warships to leeward formed a squadron under three flag officers escorting a convoy into the Mediterranean.

It was not till midday that Tourville was satisfied that he was in the presence of a convoy and its escorting squadron, and not of the Grand Fleet. The chevalier de Sainte-Maure, who had commanded the *Content* at Barfleur, had now taken and burnt two allied merchant vessels, and was able to report the escort as 27 ships strong. This figure gave an exaggerated notion of the allied strength: in ships of the line Rooke had but eight English and five Dutch. The Dutch flagship carried 84 guns, but all the rest were of the 3rd or 4th rate. Yet Rooke possessed one priceless advantage: he was still to windward. By about two hours after noon he had appreciated that he was in the presence of the whole French fleet, and had hauled to the wind. It appeared likely that only the French blue squadron under Gabaret could reach a position to join action before nightfall. Rooke stood off the land under easy sail in order to allow the Dutch and other ships to leeward of him to work up to windward, while Gabaret wasted precious time forming his squadron into line. At the same time Rooke sent word to some small merchant vessels near the coast to save themselves in neutral ports, or in Cadiz if they could reach it.

Soon after six in the evening the French opened fire on the leeward-most ships, which soon afterwards tacked towards the shore, followed by the enemy. Schryver, still commanding the *Zeeland* as at Barfleur, was at first engaged by the *Ardent*, a ship of about equal force under d'Ivry, who had also fought in the earlier action and had brought the *Modéré* safely into St Malo. D'Ivry was soon afterwards joined by Gabaret's 92-gun flagship, the *Victorieux*, and the Dutchman was forced to strike. Van der Poel in the 64-gun *Wapen van Medenblick* was similarly overwhelmed by the *Dauphin Royal* of 100 guns carrying Pannetier's flag. When darkness fell, these were the only two warships that had been lost.

Several of the merchant vessels and two small warships were mopped up in succeeding days as they vainly attempted to find sanctuary in harbour.

Much of the convoy and escort had been allowed to escape when the French tacked for the shore. Next morning Rooke found the bulk of the escort with him, as well as 54 merchant vessels. Four enemy warships were still in sight, and one came within shot. The *Royal Oak* gave her a broadside, and she crowded on sail to leeward without making reply. Rooke learned from his captains that the *Monk*, one of the escorts, had been seen to bear away southward during the night, with one Dutch warship and about 40 or 50 more sail of merchantmen. He could do nothing to save the rest, nor was there any chance of fighting his way into the Mediterranean. He therefore steered for Madeira to water the ships before returning home. At Madeira he found the *Monk* with her contingent, and the whole convoy and escort were able to sail in company for Ireland. They had the satisfaction of taking two French merchant vessels on the way. When 150 miles south-west of Cape Clear, Rooke detached the *Lark* to bear to England the melancholy news of the reverse.

William's Mediterranean squadron, which he had so much desired to see exerting a political influence in the middle sea, reached Cork on 30 July. Although many ships and cargoes of the giant convoy had escaped destruction, they had failed dismally to reach their destinations. All Europe could see that, despite the setback of the previous year, Tourville was still master of the sea routes.

There can be no doubt that the French admiral ought to have done better. Every man is, however, to some extent a prisoner of his own experience; the result of engaging a much superior fleet off Barfleur had imprinted itself very firmly on Tourville's mind. He could not risk a repetition.

There was great apprehension in London throughout the month of June. Insurance rates mounted, and some members of the Privy Council were reported to have gone to the City to re-assure the merchants, though the backing for their optimism is hard to discern. Insurance rates then started to fall, and continued to do so up to mid-July on the basis that no news is good news. Evelyn prayed that God might avert the Turkey-merchants' fleet falling into the hands of the French, but by 15 July the first letters from Lisbon had arrived, followed soon afterwards by the report brought in by the *Lark*, which had reached Dartmouth. The disaster off Cape St Vincent was accounted in the City as the severest blow since the great fire 27 years earlier.[7]

Nottingham, comparing the list of ships said to be in company with Rooke with lists from a consular report of those safe in Spanish harbours, found that the loss, though considerable and grievous, fell far short of what might have been feared. The conduct of the French fleet in this action, he concluded, must have been very ill for the allies to have escaped so lightly. About 90 merchantmen were lost, of which about 50 were destroyed and the rest captured. The greater part of this loss fell on the Dutch, and the City of London's loss, though serious, was not as great as had been feared when the first reports came in.

With no naval opposition left in the Channel, it might have been expected that this was the moment to press the long-delayed attack on the arsenal at Brest. But nothing was attempted and, as the summer came to an end, the English gave themselves up to recrimination. One of Pepys' old servants, who had sailed on board the *Britannia*, gave the former Secretary a disturbing account of the management of the fleet flagship. There had been a fire aboard when in the Bay of Biscay, and at other times the ship had been aground. The three admirals had set a bad example by sitting and drinking till the small hours of the morning, and conduct lower down was no better.

Back in harbour, the admirals found themselves assailed by searching questions about their conduct of operations. The Commissioners of the Admiralty asked on 14 July for a particular account of what had been done in execution of the sailing orders issued on 19 May. The admirals excused themselves by saying that they were not masters of the winds, and that they had no certain knowledge of the whereabouts of the French fleet; they were supported by Almonde who gave his opinion that more could not have been done. It was false reasoning. For it was at all times open to the commanders-in-chief to ascertain whether or not the French fleet was at its base. The whole operation had been bungled because they had received a report on this vital matter after they had released the convoy rather than before, and even then had no intelligence which way the enemy had gone.

It was not a reply that was likely to satisfy the merchants of the Levant company, nor the powerful Whig interests in the City. The company lost little time in presenting an address to the queen in council, relating what had occurred from the time that the convoy was agreed upon to the time it sailed, and praying Her Majesty, in terms which in the circumstances were extremely modestly drawn, to order an enquiry into any miscarriage, so that better care should be taken in future. Mary directed the whole council to assist in the enquiry, and to advise her what had gone wrong.

The Clerk of the Privy Council delivered a questionnaire to the admirals early in October. The key question was the second: 'whether it was resolved in the council of war of 22 May that if the French fleet were sailed out of Brest they could advise further what measures were to be taken before they parted with the Straits squadron?' The admirals replied that they did not remember or know of any debate on 22 May about 'taking any measures for intelligence of the French fleet being sailed out of Brest', adding that no flag officer present made any proposal of that kind, the matter having been very fully debated at the council of 15 May. A week later they were concerned only with carrying out their sailing orders.[8]

What the admirals were saying, in effect, was that on 15 May they had decided that it was unwise to sail the Straits convoy until the whereabouts of the Toulon squadron was established. When, therefore, they were told to provide the convoy with cover 'as far as a council of war should think proper', they thought only of escorting it clear to the south-westward of Ushant. If the Toulon squadron had concentrated with the rest of the enemy fleet, the convoy would then be safe from the major threat. If, on the other hand, the Toulon squadron was still on passage, the allied Straits squadron was strong enough to protect the convoy. It does not appear to have occurred to anybody that the main French fleet might have sailed southward. It had been a bold move by Tourville, and it had given him moments of anxiety as his fleet lay day after day in Lagos bay, the convoy failed to appear, and he received reports that the allies were planning a descent on the coast of France. Because of his faulty tactical handling of his fleet when his prey was at long last within reach, his well-conceived strategy had succeeded less well than it might have done.

The rights and wrongs of the admirals' conduct had still not been resolved when William returned from the Continent at the end of October. There had been another engagement of the armies, called the battle of Landen, barren of decisive results but expensive in cannon fodder. One curious result was the capture of the Duke of Berwick, and his appearance before his uncle Marlborough. George Churchill, who had left the fleet and reverted to a military rank, was also present at the battle. The allies lost Charleroi, but managed to save Liège; once again the frontier held.

The king found the Whigs in full cry. Ignorance and imbecility, they argued, were insufficient to explain the loss of the convoy; treason must therefore have been present. Their motion, that the miscarriage had been due to notorious and treacherous mismanagement, was passed in the Commons, in spite of Tory protests against inclusion of the reference to treachery. The Tories saved Delaval and Killigrew from censure, but it was obvious that both they and Shovell would have to go, and that Russell must be recalled. Russell, however, had no intention of accepting the command while Nottingham remained as Secretary of State.

William wasted no more time: when he opened Parliament early in November his mind was made up. He must turn to the Whigs. Russell was to command for the coming season, the Board of Admiralty was to be replaced, and Nottingham was to go. The Secretary of State would not resign; to have done so would have been to have admitted some responsibility for the losses that had occurred. He delivered the seals of office only at the positive command of the king, who admitted that it was only from necessity that he parted with the man who had performed so magnificently in his service. No doubt Nottingham had made mistakes and errors of judgment, or what can be seen as such by an onlooker of a later century with all the facts at his disposal. Most administrative decisions, whether of a political or a military nature, have to be made with an imperfect knowledge of all the relevant factors, often in a hurry, and above all with no idea of what fate has in store in the way of surprises. It was Nottingham's misfortune to fall a victim of political spite after over four years of devoted service and very hard work. Mary noted that the king had been forced to part with him in order to please a party which he could not trust.

With Russell back in command of the fleet and soon to become First Lord of the Admiralty, the Royal Navy was poised to play its part in making England, and from 1707 the United Kingdom, into a power of the first rank. The wheel of fortune had turned full circle many times in the first five years of the revolution: first the inability of the English to interfere with French maintenance of a hostile Ireland, then the English support, uninterrupted by the French, of the allied army sent to regain that kingdom; next the French successful application of the doctrine of the 'fleet in being' in 1689, followed by the disastrous failures of the allies to apply it in the following year, and of the French in 1692; Mary's peremptory orders to Torrington to engage a superior enemy, Tourville's receipt two years later, when much inferior to allied strength, of even firmer orders from his king; the replacement of Torrington in defeat by a commission of three, the similar replacement of Russell after a great victory not fully exploited; Tourville's failure to extract real gain from his victory at Beachy Head, Russell's inability to achieve anything after the Hogue; Tourville's failure, when in command of the Channel, to see the importance of interrupting English support of the army in Ireland, followed by Russell's failure, when the mastery was again in dispute, to realize that his main task was to isolate the Franco-Irish army from French succour; Nottingham's triumph over Russell, and Russell's final reinstatement at Nottingham's expense.

More important than these twists and turns of fate was the realization, after the loss sustained by the Smyrna convoy in 1693, that men-of-war do not exist solely to fight the enemy fleet. It began to be seen that naval power enables its possessor to use the sea for its own purposes, whether to make a descent on the enemy coast, as was planned in 1692, or to bring its merchant fleets safely to their destinations, as should have been the outcome in the next year. If the enemy fleet interferes with these operations, it must be fought, just as it must be prevented by fighting from forwarding similar operations of its own. By engaging the French at Barfleur and destroying many of their best ships at Cherbourg and la Hougue, the allied fleet prevented a Franco-Irish invasion of England and the possibility of a Jacobite rising in its support. But it was far less successful in countering the war against the merchant shipping on which both England and the Netherlands depended for their prosperity.

Four more years were to run before the Treaty of Ryswick brought the war to an end with the French king's acknowledgment that William was the rightful king of England. Rooke and Shovell, Benbow and Leake, were ready to take important commands and to make full use of their fighting experience. Russell was ready to accept a peerage as Earl of Orford and to take a fleet into the Mediterranean. There would be more mistakes, more disasters from storm and from enemy action. But there would also be more victories. Above all the kingdom was set on a course which was to be followed with varying fortune in successive wars of the eighteenth century, until it could be said, as a matter of fact rather than as a boast, that Britannia ruled the waves.

Chapter 10

Royal Hospital, Greenwich. Perspective view of Wren's original design, later much modified (The Trustees of Sir John Soane's Museum).

Memorial   *1695-1703*

John Evelyn, extracts from whose contemporary comments on events have been reproduced throughout the foregoing narrative, had earlier been a Commissioner for Sick and Wounded Seamen. A resident of Deptford and a friend of Pepys, he had first been appointed almost 30 years before the battles of Barfleur and the Hogue moved Queen Mary to undertake the building of a naval hospital. Up to that time, the best that could be arranged, when a fleet action or an epidemic outbreak produced a sudden increase of wounded or sick men from the fleet, was the reservation of half the accommodation at St Thomas's Hospital in Southwark. One of Evelyn's jobs as a commissioner was to arrange the disposal of the sick and wounded when the fleet came into harbour.

Some time before the royal initiative, the Navy Board had started to examine the provision of hospitals for seamen, and had been advised to set up six, the suggested locations being Carisbrooke and Dover castles, Liverpool, Plymouth, Chatham and Greenwich. Carisbrooke and Greenwich were inspected in the summer of 1691, but little progress had been made before the battle took place in the following year, although in February and March 1692 the Board of Admiralty was pressing the Commissioner for Sick and Wounded for early action at Greenwich. Then in October the queen decided to provide a site in the grounds of the palace at Greenwich. The Queen's House was to be maintained as a royal residence, for use by the royal family and for the entertainment of ambassadors on their arrival from oversea, before they presented their letters of credence at Court. By the autumn of 1694 some eight acres along the river front had been set aside for the hospital.

Mary was not destined to see any more progress on the scheme which she had set on foot. That winter she died from smallpox at the early age of 32. William, who had been genuinely fond of his wife and was grieved at her loss, gave instructions that the plans for Greenwich should go forward, and that the hospital for sick and wounded from the fleet should be built in memory of the queen, together with a home for pensioners and their dependants.

Thus it came about that Evelyn, though in his 75th year, was summoned by Godolphin to the Treasury on 17 February 1695, and offered the treasurership of the hospital which was to be built at Greenwich. Money for the endowment was to be found by subscription; in May the commissioners appointed to raise it got down to work with an initial meeting at the Guildhall. Evelyn, who had given up the use of his house at Deptford to his son in the previous summer, was still able to stay there while he attended to this new work, though later he took a house in Dover Street. Sir Christopher Wren, whose beautiful new cathedral would soon be rising on the site of the old St Paul's destroyed in the fire of 1666, was to give his services gratuitously as architect; he attended this first meeting, and many more that followed. He and four others formed a committee to view the site and to make recommendations.

There was already a partially completed building, known as the King's House, started during the reign of Charles II. The committee advised that it could be completed and made fit to house between 300 and 400 seamen at a cost of £6,000. The new land allocated for the hospital was divided from this building by a central avenue or vista in front of the Queen's House, which stood on slightly higher ground behind the tilt-yard. Since Wren's design envisaged two buildings of uniform appearance, one on either side of the Queen's House when viewed from the river, the committee thought that the king should be asked to grant the land between them. Finally the committee found that the water springs and conduits belonging to the ancient palace had been diverted and obstructed, and asked for their restoration as an amenity essential to the hospital.

A grand committee of 60 persons was constituted in December. Its membership contained several names that have appeared in these pages: Benbow, Evelyn, Haddock, Lowther, Pepys, Russell, Southwell and Wren. They were divided into three sub-committees with responsibility for the fabric, the constitution, and the revenue. Obviously, it was the revenue that was crucial to the success of the project.

The king had opened the list of subscriptions with a promise of £2,000, payable at Christmas. Early in January 1696 the committee found it necessary to ask him for the money as an inducement to others to pay what they had pledged. As they pointed out, nothing could be begun without cash. Again, the list of contributors contained many names familiar to readers of these pages: the Duke of Leeds (formerly Carmarthen), Pembroke, Portland and Devonshire all promised £500; Monmouth and Godolphin £200, Rooke £100.

The committee also needed some source of revenue to pay the salaries of the administrative staff, and they made various ingenious suggestions how the money might be raised. In the event the bulk came from a form of seamen's insurance, each man contributing sixpence a year, whether he was in the king's service or in that of a merchant. This money began to come in in 1697; by the end of 1699 over £36,000 had been received from all sources, and most of it had been expended. The first 100 seamen were admitted in October of that year.

On 30 June 1696 Evelyn went to Greenwich with Sir Christopher and other members of the committee, and there, 'precisely at five o'clock in the evening, after we had dined together . . . the King's astronomical professor observing the punctual time by instruments', the foundation stone was laid.[1] It makes a delightful picture: on level ground beside the river, with a summer's evening traffic of barges and wherries moving with the tide round the long bend between Blackwall Point and Limehouse Reach, the white façade of the Queen's House standing out against the summer greenery of the parkland rising behind it to the Royal Observatory, the little group of elderly men, in their newly fashionable tricorn hats, long wigs, steinkirk cravats, large cuffed coats and breeches, stockings and high-tongued shoes, counting down the seconds with all the earnestness of a later generation blasting off a manned rocket into space, as they solemnly laid a corner stone of what was to become perhaps the noblest collection of buildings in England.

Evelyn continued in office till August 1703, and spent over £89,000. As his 83rd anniversary approached, he resigned in favour of his son-in-law, who had been a member of the committee from the beginning. Building continued long after William, Wren and Evelyn were dead; the hospital was completed in 1752.

Most people, admiring Wren's stately Royal Naval College of today, fail to appreciate that it stands as a memorial to Queen Mary II, of whom they know little, or that it was her wish that it should be built in memory of the men who gave their lives to save England from invasion in the sea battles of Barfleur and the Hogue, of which they know next to nothing.

List of Abbreviations

HMC   Historical Manuscripts Commission
NHL   Naval Historical Library
NMM   National Maritime Museum
NRS   Navy Records Society
PRO   Public Record Office

Note Places of publication are given only for works published outside the United Kingdom.

Notes

Chapter 1. **Revolution** *1688*

1. James II to Lord Dartmouth, 10 December 1688: NMM MSS., LBK.
2. James II to Lord Dartmouth, 10 December 1688: quoted by S. B. Baxter, *William III* (1966), 242.
3. J. S. Tanner (ed.), *Samuel Pepys's Naval Minutes* (NRS 1926), 273.
4. S. Pepys, *Memoirs relating to the State of the Royal Navy of England* (1690), 212–14.
5. James II to Lord Dartmouth, 14 and 20 October 1688: NMM MSS., LBK.
6. James II to Lord Dartmouth, 9 November 1688: J. Dalrymple, *Memoirs of Great Britain and Ireland* (2nd edn, 1771–8), appendix part 1, 325.
7. Lord Dartmouth to Pepys, 9 November 1688: HMC Dartmouth MSS. iii 63.
8. Churchill has drawn attention to this. The rest of this passage is based on the correspondence in NMM MSS., LBK.
9. Quoted by J. Haswell, *James II, Soldier and Sailor* (1972), 284.

Chapter 2. **Consolidation** *1689*

1. Russell to Nottingham, 17 June 1692: HMC Finch MSS. iv 244.
2. NMM MSS., CAD/D/20, October 1693.
3. G. F. Duckett, *Naval Commissioners 1660–1760* (1889), 111.
4. Danby to the Princess of Orange, 4 January 1689: A. Browning (ed.), *Thomas Osborne, Earl of Danby*, vol. ii, *Letters* (1944).
5. E. B. Powley, *The Naval Side of King William's War* (1972), 112 (Herbert) and 36 (Southwell).
6. *The Diary of John Evelyn*, ed. de Beer (1959), 908: entry for 26 April 1689. Hereafter cited as Evelyn.)
7. Powley, *op. cit.*, appendix i, 370.
8. Torrington to Nottingham, 7 September 1689: quoted by Powley, *op. cit.*, 287.
9. Count Forbin, *Memoirs of the Count de Forbin, translated from the French* (2nd edn, 1734), 252.

Chapter 3. **Defeat** *1690*

1. Evelyn, 916: entry for 11 January 1690.
2. Russell to Nottingham, 2 and 7 January 1690: quoted by Powley, *op. cit.*, 327.
3. Quoted by Powley, *op. cit.*, 338n.
4. Quoted by J. Ehrman, *The Navy in the War of William III* (1953), 342.
5. Torrington to Nottingham, 26 June 1690: H. W. Hodges and E. A. Hughes, *Select Naval Documents* (1922), 90–1.
6. The queen to Torrington, 29 June 1690: *ibid.*, 92.
7. Dalrymple, *op. cit.*, appendix part 1, 112–13.
8. H. Richmond, *The Navy as an Instrument of Policy, 1558–1727* (1953), 216.
9. Evelyn, 928: entry for 6 July 1690.
10. Quoted by Dalrymple, *op. cit.*, i 433.
11. Nottingham to Southwell, 6 July 1690: NMM MSS., SOU/12.
12. Nottingham to Dursley, 14 July 1690: HMC, Downshire MSS., i part I, 356.
13. NHL, MSS., 62.
14. Evelyn, 928: entry for 17 July 1690.
15. Shrewsbury to Carmarthen, 12 July 1690: Dalrymple, *op. cit.*, ii 173.
16. The queen to the king, 22 July 1690: Dalrymple, *op. cit.*, ii, appendix part 2, 144.
17. The queen to the king, 24 July 1690: *ibid.*, 147.
18. Carmarthen to the king, 2 August 1690: A. Browning (ed.), *Thomas Osborne, Earl of Danby*, ii, *Letters*.
19. Ehrman, *op. cit.*, 354n.
20. Sir John Leake: Callender, *Life of Sir John Leake* (NRS 1920), 43.
21. J. Charnock, *Biographia Navalis* (1794), i 355.
22. H. W. Chapman, *Mary II, Queen of England* (1953), 194 and 195.

Chapter 4. **Resurgence** *1691*

1. Quoted by Ehrman, *op. cit.*, 377.
2. Evelyn, 944: entry for 19 July 1691.
3. Russell to Nottingham, 9 and 13 July 1691: HMC, Finch MSS., iii 147 and 153.
4. *Barlow's Journal* (1934), 419.
5. Russell to Nottingham, 31 July 1691: HMC, Finch MSS., iii 189.
6. *Grafton* log, 3 September 1691.
7. C. H. Firth (ed.), *Naval Songs and Ballads* (NRS 1907), 112–13.
8. HMC, Finch MSS., iii 248, quoted by Ehrman, *op. cit.*, 380.
9. J. S. Corbett (ed.), *Fighting Instructions 1530–1876* (NRS 1905), 192 and 193.
10. *Quarterly Review*, 176, 463.

11.   Evelyn, 941 and 944: entries for 11 and 19 July 1691.
12.   G. N. Clark, *The Dutch Alliance and the War against French Trade, 1688–1697* (1923), 63.
13.   Evelyn, 944–5: entries for 16 August and 14 September 1691.

Chapter 5. **Danger** *Spring 1692*

1.   Evelyn, 952: entry for Holy Week (20–6 March) 1692.
2.   Nottingham to Blathwayt, 15 March 1692: HMC, Finch MSS., iv 29.
3.   NMM MSS., WTS/30/2 and PRO, Adm. 7/692.
4.   C. de la Roncière, *Histoire de la Marine Française* (Paris 1932), 99–102.
5.   NMM MSS., SOU/13.
6.   HMC, Finch MSS., iv 85.
7.   Portland Collection, PWA 1091.
8.   HMC, House of Lords MSS., 225.
9.   Russell to Nottingham, 9 May 1692: HMC, Finch MSS., iv 133.
10.   HMC, Finch MSS., iv 114 and 142.
11.   R. Doebner (ed.), *Memoirs of Mary, Queen of England* (Leipzig, 1886), 46.
12.   Evelyn, 954: entries for 24 April and 5 May 1692.
13.   Russell to Nottingham, 2 June 1692: *English Historical Documents* (1950), viii 836.
14.   Russell to Nottingham, 5 June 1692: HMC, Finch MSS., iv 205.

Chapter 6. **Action** *19–21 May 1692*

1.   R. Allyn, *A Narrative of the Victory near la Hogue* (1744), 25.
2.   Shovell's account, printed in Allyn, *op. cit.*, 34.
3.   Russell to Nottingham, 5 June 1692: HMC, Finch MSS., iv 205.
4.   Russell to Nottingham, 4 July 1692: HMC, Finch MSS., iv 290.
5.   Portland Collection, PWA 1086.
6.   *Victory* log, 19 May 1692.
7.   Corbett, *op. cit.*, 193.
8.   *Ossory* log, 21 May 1692.
9.   *Victory* log, 22 May 1692.
10.   Russell to Nottingham, 25 May 1692: HMC, Finch MSS., iv 184.
11.   Russell to Nottingham, 5 June 1692: HMC, Finch MSS., iv 205.

Chapter 7. **Kill** *22–24 May 1692*

1.   Delaval to Nottingham, 22 May 1692: *London Gazette*, 25 May 1692.
2.   Duke of Berwick, *Mémoires du Maréchal de Berwick* (Paris 1778), 111.
3.   Dalrymple, *op. cit.*, i 508.
4.   J. C. de Jonghe, *Geschiedenis van het Nederlandsche Zeewesen* (Harlem, 1860), 314n.
5.   Russell to Nottingham, 23 May 1692: HMC, Finch MSS., iv 178.

6. N. Luttrell, *A Brief Historical Relation of State Affairs from September 1678 to April 1714* (1857), 459.
7. Nottingham to Blathwayt, 25 May 1692: NMM MSS., SOU/13.
8. Luttrell, *op. cit.*, 463.
9. Evelyn, 955: entry for 22 May 1692.
10. Firth, *op. cit.*, 123–4.
11. *Ibid.*, 124.
12. Russell to Nottingham, 27 May and 2 June 1692: HMC, Finch MSS., iv 191 and 199.

Chapter 8. **Indecision** *Summer 1692*

1. Quoted by Richmond, *op. cit.*, 228.
2. Russell to Nottingham, 25 and 27 May 1692: HMC, Finch MSS., iv 184 and 189.
3. Nottingham to Russell, 27 May 1692: HMC, Finch MSS., iv 188.
4. Luttrell, *op. cit.*, ii 467.
5. Russell to Nottingham, 13 June 1692: HMC, Finch MSS., iv 227.
6. Portland Collection, PWA 1087.
7. Russell to Nottingham, 21 June 1692: HMC, Finch MSS., iv 252–3.
8. Russell to Nottingham, 30 June 1692: HMC, Finch MSS., iv 270–1.
9. Blathwayt to Nottingham, 20 June 1692, and Portland to Nottingham, 20 June 1692: HMC, Finch MSS., iv 245–6.
10. Nottingham to Southwell, 22 July 1692: NHM MSS., SOU/13.
11. Russell to Nottingham, 3 July 1692: HMC, Finch MSS., iv 285.
12. J. Burchett, *Memoirs of Transactions at Sea* (1703), 159.

Chapter 9. **Retribution** *1693*

1. T. B. Macaulay, *History of England from the Accession of James II* (8 vols, 1885), v 2248–9.
2. Evelyn, 962–3: entries for 3 January and 5 February 1693.
3. Tanner, *op. cit.*, 289–90.
4. Portland Collection, PWA 1092, 1093, 1094.
5. NMM MSS., PHB/P/2.
6. Evelyn, 967: entry for 28 May 1693.
7. Evelyn, 968–9: entries for 21 June and 19 July 1693.
8. NMM MSS., PHB/P/2.

Chapter 10. **Memorial** *1695–1703*

1. Evelyn, 1010: entry for 30 June 1696.

Appendices

APPENDIX 1

Allied Line: Dutch squadron, 19 May 1692

Noordholland	68	de Jongh	*key:*
Zeelandia	90	Geleyn Evertsen SBN	LA luitenant-admiraal
Ter Goes	54	Martens	VA vice-admiraal
Gelderland	64	van der Scolck	SBN schout-by-nacht
Veere	62	Mosselman	
Conink William	92	van der Putte VA	
Eerste Edele	74	de Boer	
Medenblick	50	Hulschen	
Brandenburg	92	Toll	
Westvriesland	88	Muys SBN	
Zeeland	64	Schryver	
Ripperda	50	Lijnslager	
Slot Muyden	72	van der Dusse	
Prins	92	Almonde LA	
Elswoud	72	Graeff van Nassau	
Schatterschoeff	50	Wassenaer	
Leyden	64	Decker	
Princes	92	Schey VA	
Amsterdam	64	van der Saen	
Stadt es Land	50	Ross	
Veluw	64	Brakel	
Castel Medenblick	86	Callenburg VA	
Ridderschap	72	Convent	
Maegt van Doort	64	Paradys	
Capitaen Generael	84	van der Goes SBN	
Zeven Provincien	76	de Liefde	

TOTAL: 26

APPENDIX 2

Allied Line: English squadrons, 19 May 1692

RED

key:
A admiral
VA vice admiral
RA rear admiral

St Michael	90	Thomas Hopson
Lennox	70	John Munden
Bonaventure	50	John Hubbard
Royal Catherine	82	Wolfram Cornwall
Royal Sovereign	100	Humphrey Sanders: Sir Ralph Delaval VA
Captain	70	Daniel Jones
Centurion	50	Francis Wyvil
Burford	70	Thomas Harlow
Attached fireships:		*Extravagant*, destroyed at Barfleur
		Wolf, destroyed *Triomphant* at Cherbourg
		Vulcan
		Hound, expended at Cherbourg
Elizabeth	70	Stafford Fairborne
Rupert	66	Basil Beaumont
Eagle	70	John Leake
Chester	50	Thomas Gillam
St Andrew	96	George Churchill
Britannia	100	John Fletcher: Edward Russell A
		David Mitchell 1st Captain
London	96	Matthew Aylmer
Greenwich	54	Richard Edwards
Restoration	70	James Gother
Grafton	70	William Bokenham
Attached fireships:		*Flame*
		Roebuck
		Vulture
		Spy
Hampton Court	70	John Graydon
Swiftsure	70	Richard Clarke
St Albans	50	Richard Fitzpatrick
Kent	70	John Neville
Royal William	100	Thomas Jennings: Sir Cloudisley Shovell RA
Sandwich	90	Anthony Hastings
Oxford	54	James Wishart
Cambridge	70	Richard Lestock
Ruby	50	George Mees
Attached fireships:		*Phaeton*, expended at Barfleur
		Fox, expended at Barfleur
		Strombolo
		Hopewell, expended at Barfleur

TOTAL: 27

BLUE

Hope	70	Henry Robinson
Deptford	50	William Kerr
Essex	70	John Bridges
Duke	90	William Wright: Richard Carter RA
Ossory	90	John Tyrrel
Woolwich	54	Christopher Myngs
Suffolk	70	Christopher Billop
Crown	50	Thomas Warren
Dreadnought	64	Thomas Coall
Stirling Castle	70	Benjamin Walters
Attached fireships:		*Thomas & Elizabeth*, expended at la Hougue
		Vesuvius
		Hunter
		Hawk
Edgar	72	John Torpley
Monmouth	66	Robert Robinson
Duchess	90	John Clements
Victory	100	Edward Stanley: Sir John Ashby A
Vanguard	90	Christopher Mason
Adventure	50	Thomas Dilkes
Warspite	70	Caleb Grantham
Montagu	62	Simon Foulks
Defiance	60	Edward Gurney
Berwick	70	Henry Martin
Attached fireships:		*Speedwell*
		Griffin
		Etna
		Blaze, destroyed *Soleil Royal* at Cherbourg
Lion	60	Robert Wiseman
Northumberland	70	Andrew Cotton
Advice	50	Charles Hawkins
Neptune	96	Thomas Gardner: George Rooke VA
Windsor Castle	90	Earl of Danby
Expedition	70	Edward Dover
Monk	60	Benjamin Hoskins
Resolution	70	Edward Good
Albemarle	90	Sir Francis Wheeler
Attached fireships:		*Half Moon*, expended at la Hougue
		Owner's Love
		Cadiz Merchant, expended at Barfleur
		Lightning

TOTAL: 29

Also present:

Portsmouth galley	46
Charles galley	32
Mary galley	32
Greyhound	16
Saudadoes	16
Shark	4

APPENDIX 3

French Line, 19 May 1692

WHITE AND BLUE

key:
VA vice-amiral
LG lieutenant-général
CE chef d'escadre

Bourbon	68	de Perrinet	destroyed at la Hougue
Monarque	90	marquis de Nesmond CE	Brest northabout
Aimable	70	chev. de Réale	Brest northabout
Saint-Louis	64	de la Roque-Persin	destroyed at la Hougue
Diamant	60	chev. de Feuquières	le Havre
Gaillard	68	chev. d'Amfreville	destroyed at la Hougue
Terrible	80	de Sèbeville	destroyed at la Hougue
Merveilleux	90	de Mons	destroyed at la Hougue
		marquis d'Amfreville LG	
Tonnant	80	de Septèmes	destroyed at la Hougue
Saint-Michel	60	chev. de Villars	St Malo
Sans-Pareil	62	de Ferville	St Malo
Sérieux	64	marquis de Blénac	St Malo
Foudroyant	84	de Relingue CE	destroyed at la Hougue
Brillant	62	commandeur de Combes	St Malo

TOTAL: 14

WHITE

Fort	60	chev. de la Rongère	destroyed at la Hougue
Henri	64	la Roche-Allard	St Malo
Ambitieux	96	Saujon	destroyed at la Hougue
		marquis de Villette-Mursay LG	
Couronne	76	chev. de Montbron	St Malo
Maure	52	des Augers	St Malo
Courageux	58	chev. de la Luzerne	St Malo
Perle	52	chev. de Forbin	St Malo

Glorieux	64	chev. de Château-Morant	St Malo
Conquérant	84	du Magnon	St Malo
Soleil Royal	104	Desnotz: Chamelins comte de Tourville VA	destroyed at Cherbourg
Saint-Philippe	84	chev. d'Infreville	destroyed at la Hougue
Admirable	90	chev. de Beaujeu	destroyed at Cherbourg
Content	68	chev. de Sainte-Maure	St Malo
Souverain	80	marquis de Langeron CE	Brest by Channel
Illustre	70	de Combes	Brest by Channel
Modéré	52	d'Ivry	St Malo

TOTAL: 16

BLUE

Excellent	60	du Rivault-Huet	St Malo
Prince	56	de Bagneux	Brest by Channel
Magnifique	86	marquis de Coëtlogon CE	destroyed at la Hougue
Laurier	64	chev. d'Hervault	St Malo
Brave	58	chev. de Chalais	St Malo
Entendu	60	de Ricoux	wrecked at le Havre
Triomphant	76	de Machault-Belmont	destroyed at Cherbourg
Orgueilleux	94	Courbon-Blénac Gabaret LG	Brest by Channel
Fier	80	de la Harteloire	destroyed at la Hougue
Fleuron	56	chev. de Montgon	St Malo
Courtisan	64	Colbert de Saint-Marc	St Malo
Grand	84	Pannetier CE	St Malo
Saint-Esprit	74	de la Gallissonnière	St Malo
Sirène	64	duQuesne-Mosnier	St Malo

TOTAL: 14

APPENDIX 4

Shovell's line of battle for inshore operations, 23 May 1692

Greyhound	16		FS fireship
Charles galley	32		
Chester	50		
Crown	50		
Vesuvius	FS		
Eagle	70		
Oxford	54		

Hawk	FS	
Swiftsure	70	
Woolwich	54	
Flame	FS	
Resolution	70	
Strombolo	FS	
Hunter	FS	
Kent	70	
Greenwich	54	
Owner's Love	FS	
Cambridge	70	
Deptford	50	
Stirling Castle	70	
Half Moon	FS	expended 24 May
Berwick	70	
Warspite	70	
Thomas & Elizabeth	FS	expended 24 May
Dreadnought	64	

Also present:

Portsmouth galley	46
Tiger prize	42
Saudadoes	16
Shark, brigantine or half-galley	4

APPENDIX 5

Ships and armament

English ships of war throughout the sailing era were rated according to the number of guns carried. The following table shows the rating of the fleet at this period. Rates 1 to 4 were ships of the line, rates 5 and 6 were classed as frigates.

Rate	Guns	Remarks
1	96–100	mainly 100
2	84–90	mainly 90
3	60–82	mainly 70: new construction of 1692 80s and 70s
4	46–54	mainly 50
5	26–44	few available, usually 32
6	16–24	mainly 16

Tonnage was expressed in builder's measurement and was related to the estimated number of tuns (casks) of wine a ship could carry. Length gave the length of the gun deck in feet. The figures in the following table of typical ships will show the relative sizes. A 1st-rate drew about 22 feet, the others progressively less.

Rate	Ship	Tonnage	Decks	Length (ft)	Beam (ft)	Complement
1	*Britannia* (100)	1894	3	167½	48½	730–815
2	*Ossory* (90)	1307	3	161	44½	540–660
3	*Edgar* (70)	1046	2	154	40	340–470
3	*Monk* (60)	684	2	136	34½	340–470
4	*Chatham* (50)	696	1	126	34½	200–80
5	*Mary* galley (32)	462	1	127	29½	
6	*Greyhound* (16)	180	1	93	21½	

French warships were also rated, but only ships of the first three rates could lie in the line. The following table shows their principal details.

Rate	Decks	Guns	Types of guns	Complement
1	3	76–100	36/18/12- or 8-pounders	520–1050
2	2*	64–74	24/18- and less pounders	380–480
3	2	50–60	24/12-pounders	
4	2	40–6	12-pounders or less	260
5	1	about 30	8- or 6-pounders	150–80

* but some 74s had three decks

Although cannon shot could reach 2000 yards or more, the fighting range ('point blank') was 300 yards. Guns were of cast iron and muzzle loading. A 24-pounder, for example, was 11 feet long and weighed, with its mounting, 15½ hundredweight. It used a charge of 14 pounds of powder. The following table shows typical disposition of guns.

100-gun ship	lower deck	28	42-pounders (cannons)
	main deck	26	40-pounders
	upper deck	28	18-pounders (culverins)
	(including	4	16-pounders
	forecastle and poop)	14	6-pounders (sakers)
		100	

80-gun ship	gun deck	20	24-pounders
		2	18-pounders (culverins)
	upper deck	26	18-pounders

	forecastle	6	6-pounders (sakers)
	half deck	10	6-pounders
	coach	6	6-pounders
	poop	6	3-pounders
		———	
		80	

60-gun ship	gun deck	20	24-pounders
		2	12-pounders
	upper deck	22	9-pounders (demi-culverins)
	forecastle	4	6-pounders (sakers)
	half deck	10	6-pounders
	poop	2	3-pounders
		———	
		60	

It will be seen that the weight of broadside fell rapidly, from 1508 pounds from half the armament of a 100-gun ship to 615 pounds from an 80-gun ship and 408 pounds from a 60-gun ship.

(Figures adapted from J. J. Colledge, *Ships of The Royal Navy* vol. i (1969), *Samuel Pepys's Naval Minutes* (ed. J. S. Tanner) vol. i (NRS 1926), and the Sergison Papers (NRS 1949) for English, and E. H. Jenkins, *A History of the French Navy* (1973) for French ships.)

Bibliography

A. Contemporary manuscript sources

National Maritime Museum   ART/4
                                     CAD/D/20
                                     HIS/1, HIS/3
                                     LBK
                                     PHB/P/2
                                     SOU/1–2, 12–15, 19
                                     WTS/30–31
Naval Historical Library   MSS 62
Portland Collection   PWA 1086–1088, 1090–1094
Public Record Office   ADM 3/6, 3/7   Admiralty Board Minutes
                            ADM 7/692   Admiral Russell's Order
                                          Book 1692

ADM 51 series	Captains' Logs
Albemarle	55
Berwick	4124
Bonaventure	121
Breda	4130
Britannia	138
Burford	4133
Cambridge	4135
Centurion	4140
Charles galley	4142
Chatham	4146
Crown	3818
Defiance	4157
Deptford	240
Dreadnought	4170
Edgar	299
Elizabeth	4180
Expedition	327
Grafton	4201
Greenwich	4204
Greyhound	416

Hampton Court	4213
Hope	4220
Kent	4230
Lennox	3881
Lion	4241
Mary galley	4255
Monk	4263
Monmouth	4264
Montagu	4266
Neptune	3924
Northumberland	3924
Ossory	4279
Oxford	4281
Royal Oak	4318
Royal Sovereign	4320
Royal William	4321
Ruby	4322
Rupert	4325
St Michael	837
Saudadoes	3965
Stirling Castle	4355
Suffolk	4357
Swiftsure	932
Tiger prize	4371
Vanguard	4382
Victory	4384

ADM 52 series   Masters' Logs

Adventure	1
Advice	5
Chester	19
Restoration	97
St Albans	1
Warspite	112
Windsor Castle	110
Woolwich	121

ADM 67/1, 69/2   Greenwich Hospital Treasurer

Wombourne Wodehouse MSS   Lord Danby's Diary, 18–25 May 1692

B. Contemporary printed sources

'Account of the Engagement Drawn up by Sir Cloudisley Shovell's direction, some of it being wrote by himself', published in one volume with Allyn's journal.

Allyn, the Revd Richard. *A Narrative of the Victory near la Hogue* (1744).

An account of the late great victory obtained at sea. Published by Authority (1692).

Barlow. *Barlow's Journal* (1934).

Berwick, Duke of. *Mémoires du Maréchal de Berwick* (Paris, 1778).

Browning, Andrew (ed.). *Thomas Osborne, Earl of Danby*, vol. ii, *Letters* (1944).

Burchett, Josiah. *Memoirs of Transactions at Sea* (1703).

Burnet, Gilbert. *History of his own Time*. French translation in 4 vols. (The Hague, 2nd edn., 1727).

Callender, Geoffrey (ed.). *Life of Sir John Leake* (NRS 1920).

Charnock, John. *Biographia Navalis* (1794), 'Extract of Journal of Officer of the Ossory', i 361; 'Journal in Rooke's handwriting', i 405–7.

Corbett, J. S. (ed.). *Fighting Instructions 1530–1816* (NRS 1905).

De Beer, E. S. (ed.). *The Diary of John Evelyn* (Oxford University Press, 1959).

Doebner, R. (ed.). *Memoirs of Mary, Queen of England* (Leipzig, 1886).

English Historical Documents Vol. viii (1950), chap. 5 n.13.

English Historical Review 'Contemporary account', January 1892, 112–14.

Evelyn, John: see de Beer.

Firth, C. H. (ed.). *Naval Songs and Ballads* (NRS 1907).

Forbin, Count. *Memoirs of the Count de Forbin, translated from French* (2nd edn, 1734).

Grant, James (ed.). *The Old Scots Navy 1689–1710* (NRS 1908).

Historical Manuscripts Commission. *Journal of Capt. Grenville Collins: Dartmouth MSS.* iii (HMSO 1896).

——— Downshire MSS., i part I (HMSO 1924).

——— Finch MSS., iii (HMSO 1957) and iv (HMSO 1965).

——— House of Lords MSS. 1692–93 (HMSO 1894).

Hodges, H. W. and Hughes, E. A. *Select Naval Documents* (1922).

Laughton, J. K. (ed.). *Naval Miscellany*, vol. 2. (NRS 1912).

Leake, John: see Callender.

London Gazette. 16 and 25 May, 17 September 1692.

Luttrell, Narcissus. *A brief Historical Relation of State Affairs from September 1678 to April 1714* (1857).

Markham, Clements R. (ed.). *Life of Captain Stephen Martin* (NRS 1895).

Marsden, R. G. (ed.). *Documents relating to the Law and Custom of the Sea*, vol. ii (NRS 1916).

Morphew, T. (publisher) *The Life and Glorious Actions of the Rt. Hon. Sir George Rooke Kt.* (1707).

Papillon, A. F. W. *Memoirs of Thomas Papillon, of London, merchant (1623–1702)* (1887).

Pepys, Samuel. *Memoirs relating to the State of the Royal Navy of England for ten years determined 1688* (1690). See also Tanner, J. S.

Tanner, J. S. (ed.). *Samuel Pepys's Naval Minutes* (NRS 1926).

The British Archivist. 'Account in parish records of Northwood, Isle of Wight', i, 9–12.

Tourville, comte de. *Mémoires du maréchal de Tourville* (Amsterdam, 1753).

Villette-Mursay, marquis de. *Mémoires du Marquis de Villette* (Société de l'Histoire de France, 1841).

C. Secondary sources

Baxter, Stephen B. *William III* (1966).

Browning, Andrew. *Thomas Osborne, Earl of Danby* (1951).

Browning, Robert. *Poetical Works* (1896).

Bryant, Arthur. *Samuel Pepys, the Saviour of the Navy* (1938).

Calmon-Maison, J. J. R. *Le Maréchal de Château-Renault (1637–1716)* (Paris, 1903).

Campbell, J. *Lives of the British Admirals*, 4 vols. (1785).

Chapman, Hester W. *Mary II, Queen of England* (1953).

Charnock, John. *Biographia Navalis* (1794).

Churchill, Winston S. *Marlborough, his Life and Times*, 4 vols. in 2 books (1947).

Clark, George. *The later Stuarts* (1934).

Clark, G. N. *The Dutch Alliance and the War against French Trade, 1688–1697* (1923).

Clowes, W. Laird. *The Royal Navy, a History*, vol. ii. (1898).

Colledge, James Joseph. *Ships of the Royal Navy*, vol. i (1969).

Dalrymple, John. *Memoirs of Great Britain and Ireland* (2nd edn, 1771–88).

De Jonghe, J. C. *Geschiedenis van het Nederlandsche Zeewesen* (Harlem, 1860).

Dictionary of National Biography 21 vols. (1908).

Duckett, G. F. *Naval Commissioners 1660–1760* (1889).

Ehrman, John. *The Navy in the War of William III* (1953).

Erlanger, Philippe. *Louis XIV.* (English translation, London: Weidenfeld & Nicolson, 1970).

Feiling, Keith. *History of the Tory Party 1640–1714* (1924).

Hamilton, Elizabeth. *William's Mary* (1972).

Haswell, Jock. *James II, Soldier and Sailor* (1972).

Hervey, Frederick. *Naval History of Great Britain*, 5 vols. (1779).

Jenkins, E. H. *A History of the French Navy* (1973).

Jones, J. R. *The Revolution of 1688 in England* (1972).

Laughton, J. K. *Quarterly Review*, CLXXVI (1893).

—— *Studies in Naval History* (1887).

Lediard, Thomas. *Naval History of England 1066 to 1734* (1735).

Naval Chronicle. Vols. XX and XXXIII.

Macaulay, Thomas B. *History of England from the Accession of James II*, 8
   vols. (1885).
Mahan, Alfred T. *The Influence of Sea Power upon History* (1890).
Malo, Henri. *Les Corsaires Dunkerquois et Jean Bart*, 2 vols. (Paris, 1903).
Ogg, David. *England in the Reigns of James II and William III* (1955).
Powley, Edward B. *The English Navy in the Revolution of 1688* (1928).
—— *The Naval Side of King William's War* (1972).
Richmond, Herbert. *The Navy as an Instrument of Policy, 1558–1727* (1953).
Roncière, Charles de la. *Histoire de la Marine Française*, (Paris, 1932).
Sué, Eugène. *Histoire de la Marine Française sous Louis XIV* (Paris, 1858).
Troude, O. *Batailles Navales de la France* (Paris, 1867).
White, T. E. (trans.). *Rise and Progress of the Naval Power of England* (1802).
Wood, A. C. *A History of the Levant Company* (1935).

General index

Alderney race, 80, 108, 110, 125, 140
Allyn, Revd Richard, 95
Almonde, Liutenant-Admiraal Philips van, 32, 43–4, 47, 83–4, 91, 96, 111, 115–16, 122–3, 125, 161
Anna Maria of Neuburg, Queen of Spain, 38, 43–4, 154
Anne, Princess, 23, 43, 74, 87
Ashby, Vice Admiral Sir John, 36, 39, 47, 49, 53–4, 63, 78, 82, 84–5, 91, 100–2, 104, 106–11, 115–16, 123, 129, 143–5, 147
Ashton, John, 73, 78
Athlone, Earl of: see Ginkel, Godert de
Aughrim, Battle of, 69
Augsburg, League of, 17, 19, 128
Aylmer, Captain Matthew, 23, 25, 35, 57, 62, 64, 85, 118, 155

Bagneux, Captain de, 90, 98
Bantry Bay, Battle of, 30, 35–6, 39, 46, 97, 104
Barfleur, Battle of, 12, 30, 89–107, 125, 136, 144, 153, 158–60, 164, 167, 169
Bart, Jean, 40, 61, 62
Beachy Head, 22–3, 115
Beachy Head, Battle of, 30, 49–51, 53, 56, 61, 68, 73, 80, 85–6, 90, 101, 104, 163
Beaujeu, chevalier de, 114
Bedford, Duke of: see Russell, William
Bellasis, Lieut. General Sir Henry, 138, 141
Bellefonds, Marshal de, 79, 80, 116–17, 120
Benbow, Captain John, 52, 82, 86, 110, 139, 164, 168
Bentinck, William, Earl of Portland, 23, 46, 82, 105, 125, 133–4, 137, 143, 154, 168

Berkeley, George, Earl of, 23
Berkeley, Vice Admiral John, Baron, 25, 39, 155
Berry, Vice Admiral Sir John, 25–6, 53
Berwick, Duke of: see Fitzjames, James
Blathwayt, William, 77, 133, 135, 138, 143, 145
Bonrepaus, Intendant-General, 57, 78, 80, 116, 120
Boyne, Battle of, 50–1, 70, 79, 146
Brandenburg, Elector of, 23
Brest, 33, 35–40, 45, 55–6, 61, 63, 65, 68, 72, 79–83, 86, 88, 103–4, 107, 115, 123, 128, 133–9, 141–5, 147, 153, 155–8, 161–2
Browning, Robert, 110
Burchett, Josiah, 13, 82, 86
Burnet, Bishop Gilbert, 18–19, 22–3, 26, 32, 58
Butler, James, Duke of Ormonde, 23
Butler, Thomas, Earl of Ossory, 17

Cadiz, 46–7, 57, 70, 77, 156, 158–9
Callenburg, Vice Admiraal, 70, 123, 141–2
Campagne du Large, 65–6
Carlos II, King of Spain, 38
Carmarthen, Marquess of: see Osborne, Thomas
Carter, Rear Admiral Richard, 73, 80–3, 85, 95, 100–1, 110, 126, 128, 140
Cavendish, William, Earl of Devonshire, 17, 19, 45, 51, 61–2, 168
Charles I, 15, 32
Charles II, 15–19, 53, 168
Château-Renault, François Louis de Rousselet, Lieut. General, 35–7, 47–8, 83, 104, 128
Cherbourg, 12, 113, 117, 125, 153, 164
Churchill, Arabella, 15

Index of ships' names